Trouble in Store?
UK Retailing in the 1990s

TERRY BURKE
Deputy Head of Economic and Business Studies,
University of Westminster

J. R. SHACKLETON
Associate Head of Economic and Business Studies,
University of Westminster

Published by
INSTITUTE OF ECONOMIC AFFAIRS
1996

First published in January 1996

by

THE INSTITUTE OF ECONOMIC AFFAIRS
2 Lord North Street, Westminster,
London SW1P 3LB

© THE INSTITUTE OF ECONOMIC AFFAIRS 1996

Hobart Paper 130

ISSN 0073-2818

ISBN 0-255 36374-5

Typography by Stuart Blade Enterprises

Cover design by David Lucas

Cover picture supplied by Management Horizons

Printed in Great Britain by
BOURNE PRESS LIMITED, BOURNEMOUTH, DORSET
Set in Baskerville Roman 11 on 12 point

CONTENTS

FIGURES

FOREWORD

Retailing has been one of the more dynamic and innovative sectors of the British economy in recent times. Over the last 30 years, competition to meet the wants of consumers in a period of considerable social change has fundamentally altered the shape of retail markets. Increasing car ownership has made out-of-town shopping possible and indeed popular, and rising home ownership has greatly increased the 'do-it-yourself' market.

More generally, as a larger proportion of the population now undertakes paid work, consumers place a higher value on their time. Activities such as shopping and household duties must compete with working time, so their opportunity cost has increased. Ownership of labour-saving home appliances (for example, freezers and microwaves) has risen; retailers and manufacturers have responded by supplying frozen and other products which are complements to the appliances, and by speeding up the process of shopping. Improvements in information technology have spread to retailing, most obviously in rapid check-out systems. The growing use of credit cards and other forms of consumer borrowing has added to the rise in real incomes to boost spending power.

But are all the developments in retailing desirable? Concentration in the industry has certainly increased: the large retail groups which now appear to dominate the industry may have taken advantage of economies of scale and scope to achieve their present sizes but perhaps they now possess excessive market power which allows them to indulge in anti-competitive practices. And are there other problems in retailing with which the government should attempt to deal? For example, should there be curbs on out-of-town and edge-of-town shopping because of its effect on town centres and on the areas where big stores are now being located? Should opening hours be regulated, as they now are? Is there something 'inferior' about employment in retailing as compared with employment in manufacturing?

In *Hobart Paper* No.130, Terry Burke and Len Shackleton of the University of Westminster take up the challenge of addressing these key questions about British retailing. After describing trends since an early *Hobart Paper* (No.9 in 1961) by Christina Fulop, they discuss in Section III how competition has developed in retailing, pointing out the contrast between the conclusions one could draw from the old-fashioned structure-conduct-performance paradigm and more modern Chicago, contestable market and Austrian approaches. They conclude that

'...concerns about the overall market structure in UK retailing are exaggerated: although there is a fairly small number of big players with large market shares, there is a high degree of competition from both traditional and new forms of retailing' (p.88).

As for regulation, Burke and Shackleton argue for 'complete deregulation of opening hours' and see no need for more consumer protection regulation: competition among retailers to maintain high product quality standards is more effective than government mandates. On the 'central policy question of the moment' – using the planning process to restrict out-of-town and edge-of-town developments – Burke and Shackleton oppose regulation which, they claim, will benefit retailers already located in such areas and larger groups generally as well as going against consumers' revealed preferences. Environmental considerations are important, but they should apply not only to large retailers; in any case, the environmental consequences of regulating location may be adverse.

The authors' general conclusion is that retailing

'...is an efficient and innovative industry which is of great direct and indirect importance to the UK economy; the costs of interfering with its development, or trying to reverse it, are likely considerably to exceed the benefits' (p.90).

As in all IEA Papers, the conclusions are those of the authors – not of the Institute (which has no corporate view), its Trustees, Advisers or Directors. Whether or not readers agree with those conclusions, they will discover that the authors have injected much-needed economic analysis into discussion of this major sector of the British economy.

December 1995   COLIN ROBINSON
Editorial Director, Institute of Economic Affairs;
Professor of Economics, University of Surrey

THE AUTHORS

TERRY BURKE teaches consumer economics and retail strategy at the University of Westminster, where he is Deputy Head of Economic and Business Studies. He was an expert witness in the Sunday Trading prosecutions which preceded the reform of the law in 1994. His publications include (with Angela Genn-Bash and Brian Haines) *Competition in Theory and Practice* (Routledge, 1988) and (with Tony Askham and David Ramsden) *EC Sunday Trading Rules* (Butterworth, 1990).

J. R. SHACKLETON is Associate Head of Economic and Business Studies at the University of Westminster. He previously taught at Queen Mary College, University of London (now Queen Mary and Westfield College), and has worked as an economic adviser at the Department of Social Security. He has written or edited several books and monographs, including (ed., with Gareth Locksley) *Twelve Contemporary Economists* (Macmillan, 1981); *Wages and Unemployment* (Employment Research Centre, University of Buckingham, 1987); (with Terry Burke) *Sunday, Sunday: The Issues in Sunday Trading* (Adam Smith Institute, 1989); (ed.) *New Thinking in Economics* (Edward Elgar, 1990); and (with Linda Clarke, Thomas Lange and Siobhan Walsh) *Training for Employment in Western Europe and the United States* (Edward Elgar, 1985). For the IEA he wrote *Training Too Much? A Sceptical Look at the Economics of Skill Provision in the UK* (Hobart Paper No.118, 1992).

ACKNOWLEDGEMENTS

Thanks are due to Geoff Killick, Peter Urwin, Jonathan Pacey, Professor Colin Robinson and an anonymous referee for assistance or advice.

T.B.
J.R.S.

I. INTRODUCTION

In this country there are over a quarter of a million shops, employing around 2·5 million people who produce 10 per cent of the nation's Gross Domestic Product. UK retailing is a success story, with rapidly-growing productivity, considerable technical and organisational innovation and a wide range of choice available for consumers. Although retail sales growth faltered in the recent recession, over a longer time-scale retailing appears as one of our most inventive and exciting industries. Its dynamism is a product of the free market. In *Hobart Paper* No.9 (1961), Christina Fulop wrote that

> 'Retail trade in Great Britain...is...freer from interference by government, trade organisations, or trade unions than almost any other country in the world. There are few restrictions on the merchandise that retailers may sell; virtually no certificates of competence are required before a trader may start up in business; there are no compulsory trade apprenticeships for potential shop assistants; and retailers are penalised neither for their size nor for their efficiency. As a result, the emergence and expansion of new forms of retailing have not been seriously hindered.'[1]

As a result of recent liberalisation of shop opening hours, the abolition of Wages Councils and other deregulation initiatives, these words seem even truer today. But despite the apparent successes of the free market in the retail sector, there have always been critics who stress the possibility of significant market failure.

For centuries retailers have been regarded with suspicion. They have been characterised as middlemen (and women) who take a profit without adding value, often exploiting a gullible public in the process. From the Middle Ages, retailers were regulated in relation to such matters as price and weights and measures. In Victorian times, in response to accusations of

---

[1] Christina Fulop, *Revolution in Retailing*, Hobart Paper No.9, London: Institute of Economic Affairs, 1961, p.33. Fulop's excellent survey of the retail scene in the early 1960s provided us with the inspiration to write this *Hobart Paper*, and the reader will note several references to her work in the text.

adulteration of food, quality regulations were introduced, while in this century shop opening hours and locations have been the focus of attention. Furthermore, fear of the potential market power of large retailers has been a repeated theme down the years. Thus the Fulop *Hobart Paper*, and many official and private reports since then, touched on the issues of market concentration and anti-competitive practices. These remain live issues: this *Hobart Paper* brings the argument up to date by reference to both empirical evidence and new theoretical developments which have changed the ways in which economists think about such matters.

In addition, however, there has recently been increasing public debate over a number of rather different issues, including environmental and distributional concerns. It is argued, for example,

- that the move towards out-of-town retailing increases the use of cars (and thus pollution and other external costs);[2]

- that it eats up valuable greenfield locations;

- that it leads to declining and increasingly run-down city centres;[3]

- that the purchasing power of large supermarkets penalises small food producers; and

- leads (allegedly) to distorted agricultural systems in Third World countries.[4]

Current retailing trends, particularly the move towards out-of-town sites, are also claimed to penalise older, poorer and less mobile members of the population by reducing their choices and increasing their shopping and travel costs.

All these arguments suggest a continuing ambivalence towards retailers and, in some quarters at least, an undiminished appetite for regulation of this important area of

---

[2] See Hugh Raven and Tim Lang (with Caroline Dumonteil), *Off our Trolleys?*, Institute for Public Policy Research, 1995.

[3] House of Commons Environment Committee, *Shopping Centres and their Future*, London: HMSO, October 1994.

[4] See, for instance, the letter by Colin Spencer to *The Guardian* (25 February 1995), discussed in Section V (below, p.83).

economic activity. The highly visible retail sector of the 1990s may be storing up trouble for itself by its very success, if public perceptions of the basis of this success are (as we believe) somewhat distorted by pressure groups and media concern. This *Hobart Paper* therefore surveys a range of actual or potential public policy issues which arise in retailing, within the context of an overview of the changing nature of the sector, and critically assesses the case for renewed government intervention.

II. TRENDS IN UK RETAILING

Retailing is the process by which goods and services are sold to final consumers. This process has always been open to change. One hundred years ago it was the explosive expansion of small-scale local branch trading, pioneered by Thomas Lipton, which astonished contemporaries. In a variety of ways the pace of change is accelerating in Britain, perhaps to a greater extent than in most other European countries.

In 1961 Christina Fulop identified several emergent trends as the free market of the late 1950s replaced controls left over from the Second World War. She commented on the rise of pre-packing; self-service; supermarkets; voluntary purchasing groups; automatic selling by slot machines; mail order; discount stores and consumer associations. Some of these have gained in scale and significance: pre-packing and self-service are, for example, now virtually universal in most parts of the sector. Others, however, such as automatic selling and consumers' associations, have not lived up to their initial promise. In the case of discounting, the potential spotted by Fulop has only very recently begun to be realised in this country. Mail order has not been a particularly dynamic area; its share of retail spending has fallen in recent years. However, as explained later (pp.28-33), it may be that the advent of new technology will revive interest in the field of 'home shopping'.

Social and Economic Change

One reason why it is always impossible to forecast the pattern of retailing with any accuracy is that it will reflect the influence of wider social and economic change which must inevitably be difficult to foresee. Certainly, looking back at the last 30 years, there are many social changes which have shaped the retail environment. Some are fairly obvious:

- Rising real incomes have increased car ownership[1] and thus mobility, opening up the possibility of profitable out-of-town retailing on US lines.

---

[1] Car ownership rose in Great Britain by almost 70 per cent between 1971 and 1992. Over the same period the proportion of households with regular use of a

- Higher incomes also mean ownership of refrigerators is almost universal, and that of freezers[2] is heading the same way. This has altered food shopping patterns dramatically, with a fourfold increase in consumption per head of frozen foods taking place between 1971 and 1993.

- Home ownership has risen to historically high levels, with 16 million owner-occupied dwellings today[3] as against only 10 million in the early 1970s, helping to create an important new do-it-yourself (DIY) retail sector virtually from scratch.

- In the last two decades, the growing to maturity of the 'baby-boom' generation has unleashed an unprecedented amount of spending on clothing, leisure goods and new types of food as lifestyles have undergone rapid change.

- This has gone hand-in-hand with an explosion of advertising and new media which has tended to homogenise tastes across the nation and reduced the regional and local differences in patterns of consumption which, until recently, were still of great significance.

More subtly, the rise of institutional savings through company and personal pensions has altered saving and spending patterns, as has the spread of credit cards and other forms of consumer borrowing. By 1994, 40 per cent of people aged 18 and over held credit cards. In addition, there were in 1994, up to 15 million retail credit accounts, mainly in the form of store cards.[4]

A much larger proportion of women goes out to work (indeed, almost half the work-force is now female), while the average size of household has fallen from 2·9 in 1971 to 2·4

---

car rose from 52 per cent to 68 per cent (Department of Transport, *Transport Statistics: Great Britain*, 1994 edition).

[2] Ownership of a deep freeze or fridge freezer rose from 49 per cent in 1981 to 87 per cent in 1993 (Central Statistical Office, *Social Trends*, 1995 edition).

[3] 66 per cent of homes in Great Britain were in owner-occupation in 1993. (*Annual Abstract of Statistics*, 1995.)

[4] Data from the Credit Card Research Group. The market leaders in retailers' own cards are Marks & Spencer and the Burton Group, each of which have around three million cardholders. ('Shop till you drop', *International Journal of Retail and Distribution Management*, Vol.23, No.3, 1995, page vi.)

today. The amount of time available for shopping has therefore changed; while non-working women spend on average 4·56 hours per week shopping for groceries, working women spend only 2·93 hours.[5] Thus the appeal of the 'one-stop-shopping' offered by large food retailers such as Sainsbury's and Tesco has increased, generating a growing demand for convenience products like the ready-prepared meals which have proved so profitable for Marks & Spencer and other retailers. Between 1983 and 1993 consumption of all convenience foods rose by 10 per cent. As the pattern of shopping shifted to concentrate on weekends, lunchtimes and evenings, pressure for reform of shopping hours was inevitable. The consequent extension of opening hours has, of course, itself been facilitated by increasing use of part-time (particularly female) employees in retailing, again part of a larger picture of changing work patterns and greater labour market flexibility.

Another feature of wider social change which has significantly affected UK retailing is the growth of ethnic minority businesses over the last 30 years. Retailing is an important sector of self-employment. In the late 1980s the Labour Force Survey showed that, amongst ethnic minority self-employed, 36 per cent were engaged in retailing; the proportion was over 50 per cent for those of Indian origin. By contrast, only 11 per cent of white self-employed were in retailing. In some parts of Britain (especially in London and the South East, West Yorkshire and the West Midlands) small retailing outlets, especially in food and confectionery, newspapers and tobacco, are dominated by Asian and other ethnic minorities.[6]

---

[5] Study by the Henley Centre, reported in *The Independent*, 24 March 1995.

[6] Such enterprises are likely to be very small, relying heavily on informal sources of capital and making much use of family labour. They display low productivity and owners typically work very long hours. For example, one study (Trevor Jones, David McEvoy and Giles Barrett, 'Success or just survival?', *New Economy*, Spring 1994, pp.51-56) showed average Asian owners of such small businesses working 60·4 hours per week as against 47·3 hours for their white counterparts. However, retailing represents an important means by which ethnic minorities can enter business life when other avenues may be blocked by discrimination or lack of appropriate qualifications or connections, and the extended opening hours of small corner grocery stores played a part in encouraging the multiples to follow suit.

Changes in population location have also occurred. As in the USA, there has been a move towards the suburbs and the countryside predominantly by the more affluent which, together with increasing levels of crime and vandalism in inner cities,[7] has reduced the attractiveness of traditional shopping areas. Consequently, the number of out-of-town shopping malls, mainly for car-based shoppers, increased in number dramatically in the late 1980s (see Figure 1), though expansion has tailed off recently. One sign of the times is that in 1993 London's Oxford Street was Britain's premier trading location in terms of turnover, but a year later it came only fourth behind Meadowhall in Sheffield, the Metro Centre in Gateshead and Merry Hill in Dudley – all examples of the new type of purpose-built mall.

Continuing Growth of Large Multiples

Over the 1980s all these factors contributed to a rapidly growing and changing pattern of retailing. The value of retail spending rose by more than 40 per cent in real terms. The fastest-growing areas were DIY and furniture and furnishings, though food sales also grew faster than retailing as a whole (see Table 1). Over this period total employment rose only slightly; however, the composition of the work-force altered significantly as the number of part-timers rose, and output-per-hour worked in the sector rose by around 50 per cent.

In the recession of the early 1990s, retailing growth as a whole was sluggish, although food sales continued to grow. The recession accentuated a longer-term tendency towards concentration in retailing (especially in food retailing, which accounts for nearly 40 per cent of the sector's revenue).[8]

For many years, 'multiples' – firms with more than one shop – have increased in importance. In retail grocery, for instance, the multiples' 20 per cent market share in the 1950s had doubled by the late 1960s and continued to grow steadily

---

[7] A recent study by Sheffield University has revealed that teenagers increasingly fear town centres and prefer to shop in 'clean and safe' out-of-town shopping malls: 'Shopping malls win youth vote', *The Times Higher Education Supplement*, 28 July 1995.

[8] Total UK turnover for food, drink and tobacco was £65,302 million in 1993, out of a total retail turnover of £148, 529 million. (*UK Service Sector Retailing*, CSO, 1995.)

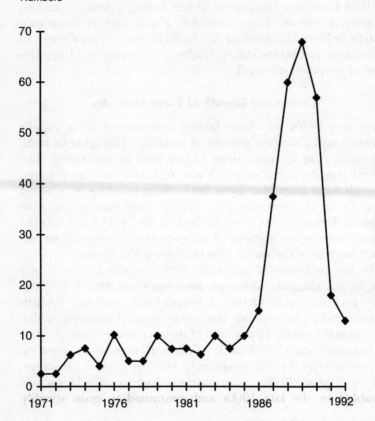

FIGURE 1: Out-of-Town Shopping Developments[1] in the United Kingdom, 1971-92

Numbers

[1] Number of developments completed each year over 5,000 square metres or 50,000 square feet.

Source: Social Trends.

TABLE 1:
Growth in Value of Retail Sales at Current Prices, 1984-94
(1980 = 100)

Description	1984	1989	1994
All Businesses	138	208	266
Food	139	200	274
Clothing and Footwear	132	215	254
Furniture and Furnishing	133	217	296
Electrical Goods	141	192	220
DIY	166	374	478
Miscellaneous	141	210	255

Source: Business Monitor.

through the 1970s and 1980s.[9] Not surprisingly, the larger multiples have grown in relative importance. In 1976 large multiples (those with a turnover of more than £5 million) accounted for 51·4 per cent of all retailing turnover; by 1991 the proportion accounted for by large firms had risen to 63·0 per cent. For food retailing the figures are 50·3 per cent and 78·8 per cent respectively.[10]

These figures conceal an even more marked concentration in the hands of a small number of major players. While the largest 10 enterprise groups accounted for 22 per cent of retail trade in 1982, this had risen to 33·9 per cent by 1993. In food retailing, where the number of outlets fell sharply (from 82,625 to 64,000) over this period, concentration has become very marked indeed. By 1991 two companies (Sainsbury's and Tesco) accounted for 32·9 per cent of the market in the UK. This puts them both in the world's top 25 retailers, as Table 2 illustrates – although they have some way to go before they rival giants like the USA's Wal-Mart or Germany's Metro.

Economies of Scale and Scope

A key feature in the increasing importance of the large players is the growth of the average size of outlet. One much-discussed aspect of this is the spread of hypermarkets and superstores,

[9] Peter Jones, 'The growing importance of Price in the Retail Marketing Mix', *Economics and Business Education*, Winter 1994, p.143.

[10] Own calculations; data from *Business Monitor*.

TABLE 2:
The World's Leading Retailers, by Sales

Retailer	Main Type of Trade	Home Country	Sales 1993 $bn	Annual Average % Change 1988-93	Number of Stores 1993	Annual Average % Change 1988-93
Wal-Mart	Discount	USA	68·0	26·7	2,540	13
Metro Int.	Diversified	Germany	48·4	19·1	2,750	na
Kmart	Discount	USA	34·6	5·6	4,274	0·1
Sears, Roebuck	Department	USA	29·6	–0·5	1,817	2·0
Tengelmann	Supermarket	Germany	29·5	8·2	6,796	6·8
Rewe Zentrale	Supermarket	Germany	27·2	13·2	8,497	2·2
Ito-Yokado	Diversified	Japan	26·0	19·4	12,462	25·2
Daiei	Diversified	Japan	22·6	10·5	5,920	12·9
Kroger	Supermarket	USA	22·4	3·3	2,208	0·1
Carrefour	Hypermarket	France	21·7	16·0	647	17·9
Leclerc, Centres	Hypermarket	France	21·1	11·1	524	1·3
Aldi	Supermarket	Germany	20·9	23·9	3,435	na
Intermarché	Supermarket	France	20·7	12·0	2,890	14·6
J. C. Penney	Department	USA	19·6	4·2	1,766	–0·4
Dayton Hudson	Discount	USA	19·2	9·5	893	8·6
American Stores	Supermarket	USA	18·8	0·3	1,695	–2·4
Edeka Zentrale	Supermarket	Germany	17·9	8·2	11,670	–2·7
Promodes	Hypermarket	France	16·0	15·6	4,676	16·0
J. Sainsbury	Supermarket	Britain	15·9	12·2	514	5·8
Jusco	Diversified	Japan	15·8	15·3	2,452	25·0
Price/Costco	Warehouse Club	USA	15·5	20·2	200	18·9
Safeway	Supermarket	USA	15·2	2·3	1,078	–1·2
Koninklijke Ahold	Supermarket	Holland	14·6	14.5	2,152	14.4
Otto Versand	Mail Order	Germany	14·4	13·6	na	na
Tesco	Supermarket	Britain	12·9	12·0	430	2·8

Source: The Economist, 4 March 1995.

mainly located at the edge of or outside towns. Although the number of such stores (defined as having 2,300 square metres [about 7,546 square feet] or more of sales space) in the UK is still below that in either France or Germany, growth in this type of retailing has been much faster since 1980 than in those countries (Table 3).[11] The leap in the scale of operation which

---

[11] This rapid growth of superstores continued into the 1990s, with other sources putting the number of such outlets at over 900 in 1994.

TABLE 3:
Number of Hypermarkets and Supermarkets: Selected European Countries, 1980-92

	1980	1981	1982	1983	1984	1985	1986	1987	1988	1989	1990	1991	1992
Belgium	79	80	81	82	86	86	88	88	88	98	110		
Denmark	29	30	36	38	38	42	42	44	44	49	50		
France	421	447	482	515	553	585	629	686	747	807	851	914	
W. Germany	813	840	860	880	910	1,522	1,561	1,572	1,583	1,635	1,656	2,056	
Italy							45	49	64	86	103	118	
Holland	37	39	37	35	34	35	35	35	35	36	38		
Spain	34	38	48	58	62	80	89	100	108	121	130	149	
UK	239	280	318	348	377	403	439	464	507	580	644	733	835

Notes: Belgium 1990: Estimated.
Denmark: All data estimated except 1980.
Figures for France and Italy are Hypermarkets only.
West Germany 1981-84 estimated.

Sources: Retail Trade Associations, National Statistical Offices, Euromonitor.

this implies is usefully illustrated by figures from Sainsbury's. In 1960 the average size of new store opened by the company was 5,800 sq.ft. (539 sq.m.); by 1980 it had increased to 14,800 sq.ft. (1,375 sq.m.) However, the average store opened in 1990 had an area of 32,300 sq.ft. (about 3,000 sq.m.).[12]

Larger sites offer clear benefits to firms[13] in terms of the range of goods on offer, stockholding economies and greater flexibility in the use of labour.[14] But the advantages of being a large player do not simply relate to the size of a given retailing site. The great economist Alfred Marshall saw this at the turn of the century. In his *Principles of Economics*[15] he wrote that 'the retail trade is being transformed, the small shopkeeper is losing ground daily'. Marshall listed the advantages of size to a retailer, including buying on better terms, cheaper delivery to the stores and specialisation of the management function. The large retailer also engages in active buying from producers, and thus 'often dispenses with middlemen between him and the manufacturer'. Multiples are able to economise on stockholding by concentrating stocks at central depots for distribution to branches.

In today's retail environment we can add other advantages of size such as specialised buying expertise and sophisticated market research which facilitate a better match of product characteristics, including price, to consumers' needs. Professional buyers can adapt the mix of products to meet shifts in

---

[12] From the Sainsbury publication, *The Best Butter in the World*, London: Ebury Press, 1994.

[13] The corollary of this is the benefit to shoppers. This is not just – or even primarily – price saving. Perhaps more importantly, a shop with large ranges of goods, including in-store bakeries, butchers and fish counters, etc., 'saves the expenditure of time which goes with traditional shopping in which the buyer buys from many sellers...It also saves the costs associated with "shopping around"'. (C.J. Bliss, 'A Theory of Retail Pricing', *Journal of Industrial Economics*, Vol.XXXVI, No.4, June 1988, p.378.)

[14] Small shops may need one or two staff, however many customers are present; for large parts of the day staff may be under-utilised. Larger shops can vary the total amount of staff employed in relation to fluctuations in demand, and can redeploy staff, for example, from checkouts to checking stock, filling shelves and carrying out maintenance.

[15] Alfred Marshall *Principles of Economics*, 8th edn., London: Macmillan, 1920 (reset 1949), pp.239-41.

consumer demand, often working closely with manufacturers and suppliers. Small store buyers may have only relatively limited expertise, stock narrower ranges, and will have to rely on manufacturers to adapt existing product lines, or bring on new versions. Professional buyers in large firms can match the production expertise of suppliers, so enabling attainment of consistent quality – as witnessed by the success of firms such as Marks & Spencer.

Furthermore, large-scale operators can use marketing and public relations to build strong reputations, creating a constituency of loyal customers who put a general trust in quality ahead of price. They can launch own-label products manufactured to their own specifications in terms of characteristics, delivery and price, while most small store buyers have to rely on branded goods. As Table 4 indicates, own-label products are particularly strongly developed in UK food retailing; apart from accounting for 100 per cent of Marks & Spencer's sales, they are 65 per cent of Sainsbury's and 50 per cent of Tesco's.[16] They are one reason for the higher average margins obtained by food retailers in this country compared with their Continental counterparts.

The benefits of size are also reflected in *economies of scope* – cost advantages arising from exploiting resources and reputation used in one economic activity in some distinct but related area. Thus Marks & Spencer used marketing and purchasing skills, together with information on customer spending patterns, to diversify from food and clothing in the 1980s into household furnishings and, more interestingly, financial services.[17] Such diversification is not always successful, of course: cautionary examples include the unhappy attempts by clothes retailer Next to move into a variety of new areas, including mail order sales. But other things equal, a large retailer moving into a new field will tend to have advantages which smaller new entrants lack.

---

[16] *Source:* David Parker and Nigel Tree, *The Business Year 1993-94*, Business Studies Magazine, 1994, p.4. 83 per cent of milk sales, 78 per cent of wrapped bread, 62 per cent of fruit juices and 55 per cent of fizzy drinks are own-label.

[17] The house credit card (Marks & Spencer still refuses to accept generic cards such as Visa, Access and Mastercard) provided the marketing platform for personal loans. The next step was to offer products to savers as well as borrowers – initially unit trusts, but extending into Personal Equity Plans.

TABLE 4:
Retailers' Own Brand Shares in Food Retailing, 1981-90
(% of total food sales)

	1981	1985	1990
Belgium	16	16	18
France	19	19	20
West Germany	5	10	16
Italy	5	7	8
Netherlands	13	21	27
United Kingdom	17	25	36

Source: Euromonitor.

Information Technology

Even the most casual of visitors to supermarkets will be aware
of the rapid development of EPOS (Electronic Point of Sale)
equipment. Computer-readable bar codes have been around
for some time,[18] but their use grew very rapidly in the late
1980s, as Table 5 demonstrates. By 1992, the UK was amongst
the heaviest users of bar-code scanners in Europe. In grocery
stores, for instance, 69 per cent of total turnover was scanned,
compared with 60 per cent in France, 38 per cent in Italy and
29 per cent in Germany.

For small firms, the benefits of EPOS have mainly been
limited to more rapid and accurate billing at check-out
counters, and improved stock control. The benefits to larger
firms are much more substantial. They include just-in-time
delivery, with consequent reductions in stockholding[19] and

---

[18] Indeed, they reflect a fairly 'low-tech' approach, as bar-codes have only a limited
informational content, offer no protection against shoplifting (for which a
separate technology, Electronic Article Surveillance (EAS) has grown up), and
represent no added value to the consumer. A large number of patents has
recently been taken out for new systems of 'intelligent tags' which will, for
example, enable goods such as video recorders to be uniquely coded with the
purchaser's name, signal maintenance dates for consumer durables and
facilitate remote diagnosis of defective products – as well as serving the
functions of existing bar-codes and EAS systems. (See 'Intelligent tagging', *Retail
Business*, Economist Intelligence Unit, No.442, December 1994, pp.3-10.)

[19] As a result of exploiting advances in information technology, 'Tesco...has cut
the amount of stock in its distribution chain to just two weeks' supply – the
lowest for any food retailer anywhere...in five years' time it could be operating
with only a week's supply'. ('Change at the Check-out: a Survey of Retailing',
The Economist, 4 March 1995, p.6.)

TABLE 5:
Number of UK Stores Employing Bar-Code Scanning, 1982-92

1982	41
1983	83
1984	185
1985	520
1986	793
1987	843
1988	2,792
1989	3,999
1990	6,043
1991	7,869
1992	9,000

Source: Euromonitor

transport costs, computer modelling to anticipate sales patterns, and the ability to choose the appropriate degree of centralisation or decentralisation of ordering to take account of local variations in demand patterns. Also, client-server networks increasingly enable manufacturers to match their week-to-week production of, for example, own-brand products to fluctuations in demand. Here again, leading British retailers seem to be in the forefront. By the end of 1992 there were 15,600 European retailers using electronic data interchange: over half were British.[20]

Another information technology development is client database marketing. Tesco's new Clubcard (which gives regular users of their stores discounts linked to total purchases) provides a wealth of information about buying patterns which can be used to target consumers.[21] It can register which products they buy, how often, at what times, in which combinations – and how customers react to price changes, methods of display, advertising and so on. Such information would be extremely costly to acquire in other ways. Other major food retailers are likely to follow this

---

[20] See J. Bamfield, 'The adoption of electronic data interchange', *International Journal of Retail and Distribution Management*, Vol.22, No.2, 1994, pp.3-11.

[21] See Jill Papworth, 'Secret weapon to tap into consumer taste', *The Guardian*, 27 May 1995.

initiative, especially as the Clubcard (although so far offering only very modest savings to regular shoppers) seems to have been the decisive factor in edging Tesco's sales ahead of its chief rival (Sainsbury's) from the Spring of 1995.[22]

Although the general tendency of these developments is to increase the average scale of operations, it should be emphasised that, by increasing the flexibility of retailing logistics, information technology may also make previously uneconomic small-scale operations profitable. Thus, after a decade in which average store size seemed to be growing inexorably, some of the large players have now begun to open rather smaller stores. For instance, Tesco has new 'Metro' stores in London's Oxford Street and Covent Garden. And the dramatic reduction in the cost of computing power is enabling some large food retailers to use smaller local suppliers once again.

Discounting

As foreshadowed in Fulop's *Hobart Paper*, an important development in several retail areas is the significant growth in discounting. Although seasonal and cyclical price discounting has existed for many years, the recession of the early 1990s seems to have taken discounting to unprecedented levels and given it new forms. This is most obvious in grocery retailing, where, with 1,300 discount stores, profit margins of mainstream operators are in decline.[23]

In the 1980s leading firms, such as Sainsbury's, Tesco and Marks & Spencer, seemed to be moving inexorably upmarket, widening their ranges to import exotic and previously virtually unobtainable fruits and vegetables and developing new high-value-added speciality convenience foods. This was designed to appeal to upwardly-mobile households, and was an important factor in maintaining profit margins for the big UK grocery chains which, while varying over the business cycle, appear on average significantly higher than those of their equivalents elsewhere in Western Europe.[24] But this strategy runs the risk

---

[22] *The Grocer*, 24 June 1995. Verdict Research (January 1996) gives Tesco's share as 14·4 per cent as against Sainsbury's 12.9 per cent.

[23] *The Times*, 8 January 1996.

[24] *The Economist*, 23 February 1991 and 4 March 1995. For further discussion, see Section III.

of neglecting the interests of many poorer consumers whose spending is, of necessity, confined mainly to a limited range of cheaper staple foodstuffs, and to whom the attractions of huge out-of-town stores may be less apparent.

For some time the UK-based Kwik Save, with around 850 stores nationwide, has pursued a different strategy from the other major players. Selling only around 1,000 product lines (less than one-fifteenth of the number stocked by a Sainsbury's superstore), and offering branded goods at prices some 10 per cent cheaper than the major multiples, Kwik Save gained market share rapidly in the early 1990s, although it has been struggling more recently. It was joined by specialist discounters from the Continent – the German Aldi (which by 1994 had 100 stores in Britain) and the Danish Netto. The latter aimed to be the cheapest discount store and claimed to offer price savings of up to 30 per cent, achieved by very basic merchandising and profit margins of 1 per cent or so as against the 7-10 per cent of the major UK multiples.

Such deep discounting stimulated a price response from the market leaders, which developed inexpensive own-label 'essentials' competing with the down-market newcomers. They also launched their own discount stores, such as Sainsbury's Bulksava and Gateway's Food Giant. This tendency towards discounting and price cutting was not confined to food retailing; similar trends can be discerned in sectors as various as clothing, footwear, do-it-yourself, household goods and bedding.[25]

A related trend, based on practice in the United States, has been the development of warehouse clubs such as that opened by Costco at Thurrock in Essex. The idea is to make available a limited range of leading branded products from large sheds to club 'members' who may be final customers or small retailers. These goods include groceries (available only in bulk packs rather than single items), electrical goods, shoes, motor accessories and office furniture. Staffing levels and promotional costs of warehouse clubs are very low, accommodation is cheap and turnover is aimed to be so rapid that stockholding is funded by trade credit from manufacturers alone. It has been estimated that these clubs could take as much as 1·5-2 per cent of total retail sales in the

---

[25] Peter Jones, *op. cit.*, pp.144-45.

years to come,[26] particularly if they are excluded (as 'industrial sites') from attempts by local planners to restrict the growth of out-of-town retailing. However, progress so far has been erratic. Nurdin and Peacock's 'Cargo Club' operation, for example, closed in March 1995 after a year of substantial losses; its sites were sold to Sainsbury's.

Another discounting model which has begun to make its mark in the UK is the factory outlet, where manufacturers sell directly to the public at significantly lower-than-normal prices. Again, this model has roots in the USA where almost 500 manufacturers have opened such outlets. The most developed version of the factory shop in Britain is in the West Country village of Street, Somerset,[27] where Clarks Shoes has created a shopping village on US lines with two Clarks outlets plus others from Laura Ashley, Jaeger, Benetton, Royal Worcester, and so on. It is attracting nearly 2 million visitors a year, for whom this sort of shopping is primarily a leisure activity rather than a utilitarian exercise.

Freeport Leisure, Hornsea, North Hull, provides another example of shopping facilities being mixed with those for leisure. Nationally known retailers offer heavily discounted goods, while Freeport provides restaurants, crazy golf and an adventure playground. In 1994 Hornsea attracted 1·4 million visitors, prompting the company to attempt a repeat of its success at Fleetwood Old Port, near Blackpool.[28]

In general, goods offered in 'factory shops' are either superseded lines or 'seconds'. While the concept is interesting, there is probably scope only for a couple of dozen such out-of-town villages of factory shops. Their effect on retailing in general is likely to be marginal, although their mere existence tends to constrain the behaviour of existing retailers.

Home Shopping?

Christina Fulop saw possibilities for expansion of one form of home shopping, mail order. In 1991 mail order accounted for about 2·7 per cent of total retail sales in the UK – a relatively

---

[26] *Ibid.*

[27] John Dawson, 'Suddenly, Street's ahead', *Daily Telegraph*, 29 March 1994.

[28] 'They do like to shop beside the seaside', *Sunday Times*, 4 June 1995.

low figure compared with that for some other countries: in West Germany in the same year, the proportion was 6·0 per cent. The potential for further growth has always been there, but it now seems likely that future expansion of home shopping will rely on more advanced technologies than the public mail system.[29] Today's telecommunications and video technology have the power, using computerised information systems, to put consumers into direct contact with suppliers, removing the need for consumer access to retail premises – whether in the High Street or on the edge-of-town, shopping mall or warehouse shed. Perhaps appropriately, Amstrad has recently decided to concentrate its activities on selling electrical products directly to the public in this way rather than relying on retailers. Interactive computing promises to provide the next wave of distance selling, expanding on the home shopping base built by catalogue, direct mail, press and TV advertising, and telephone sales.

The telephone was traditionally used in the UK and the USA to sell financial products, although in the UK the majority of unsolicited phone calls currently concern double glazing and other home improvement services. Whilst telephone installation has risen substantially (42 per cent of households had phones in 1972; 90 per cent have them today), telephone sales as such have not become a major selling medium. They can entail a violation of privacy: in Germany and Austria telephone sales are virtually outlawed on grounds of privacy and data protection. There are also potential problems of fraud, as the consumer has little evidence that the service on offer actually exists.

Television shopping channels are a fairly recent development outside the USA. The structure of the TV home shopping sector is largely determined by the national regulatory framework, with its specific mix of public and private channels. However, access to satellite channels creates opportunities for global retailing: whole programmes, indeed whole channels, as opposed to single advertisements, are devoted to shopping. Orders are usually placed and paid for

---

[29] The major mail order companies, such as Littlewoods, used to rely heavily on selling through agents who took orders amongst their friends. This type of business has been declining rapidly in favour of more privatised lifestyles where individuals buy only for themselves and their families – a trend likely to accelerate as distance shopping becomes linked to newer technologies.

over the telephone, although the technology exists for using a more advanced interactive videotext system.[30] With such a system, information providers feed data into a central computer, which is accessed by subscribers via a dial-up telephone line, with the information appearing on their TV screen or computer terminal.

In Orlando, Florida, and San Francisco, California, trials are being held with 5,000 households able to use their TV screens to browse through electronic catalogues, with access to 250,000 products (many at discount prices). Unlike existing home shopping TV channels the consumer is in charge of what appears on the screen.[31]

Major UK retailers, including Dixons, W.H. Smith, Tesco and Great Universal Stores, are planning to offer their products via CompuServe, the world's largest commercial on-line information and shopping service. Currently, CompuServe's 100,000 UK members pay £6·50 a month for a basic service which enables them to browse through an electronic catalogue and pay for chosen items by credit card. Microsoft, the computer software firm, is planning a similar home shopping network for owners of personal computers using 'Windows 95'.

At present home shopping focuses on occasional purchase items – computers, clothing, jewellery and toys – but the main potential may lie in regular food retailing for canned and packaged staples. One Illinois firm, Peapod, already offers customers a computer-based ordering and delivery service, although currently only at a premium price. It is thought that a cheaper service, sourced from warehouses rather than the local supermarkets which Peapod uses, will shortly become available.

Sainsbury's are experimenting in London with a home delivery service: shoppers select goods from a catalogue, order by telephone (or, soon, by computer), paying a £4 surcharge for next-day delivery. Tesco have been running a home delivery scheme in Gateshead for the past 12 years in conjunction with the social services.[32]

---

[30] Lydia Arossa, 'Software and Computer Services', *OECD Observer*, No.151, April/May 1988.

[31] 'The interactive bazaar opens', *The Economist*, 20 August 1994.

[32] 'Supermarket checks out shopping by phone', *The Independent*, 11 January 1996.

Competition from interactive shopping is likely to change relationships between manufacturers and their consumers, who will have to rely primarily on manufacturers' brand information. Customers may, however, still prefer to visit reputable stores, where they can see and feel products before purchase. So long as retailers make the shopping environment sufficiently attractive and sustain their reputations for offering good quality at fair prices, consumers seem unlikely to prefer the convenience of armchair shopping to the security of personal inspection.

Home shopping, whether by catalogue, telephone sales or videotext, suffers from the disadvantage that goods cannot be directly inspected. Goods are delivered from the supplier to the customer's home. In one sense, that is a convenience, but in another it is a nuisance for those households whose members go out to work. Extensive delays between purchase and consumption further reduce the expected utility of the purchase. Lack of contact between shopper and seller can open the door to misunderstanding, if not deliberate fraud. Complaints[33] centre round excessive delays in delivery, problems over quality, guarantees and difficulty in returning goods and obtaining refunds. With satellite transmission there may also be problems over the enforcement of local legal consumer rights in the jurisdiction covering the supplier.

So far distance selling, across Europe, occupies a small but significant niche. It may, however, be about to develop a life of its own as homes increasingly gain access to deregulated 'intelligent telecommunications systems'.[34] But is such a challenge to conventional retailing likely to be mounted on any scale? Certainly three of the players – retailers, network operators and payments systems – are already experimenting with putting a range of products on the Internet.[35] Technical

---

[33] For example, to the Advertising Standards Authority. In 1994 there were 409 complaints over mail order. Advertisements for health-related products seem particularly troublesome.

[34] Erich Linke, 'New Home Shopping Technologies', *OECD Observer*, October/November 1992, pp.17-19.

[35] So far with little success. 'Argos's shop on the Barclay Square "virtual shopping mall" on the Internet has performed poorly since its launch a few months ago. Mike Smith, the chief executive, said Argos had sold "hardly anything" on the Internet so far.' ('Argos escapes retail gloom on high street', *The Independent*, 15 August 1995.)

security problems over payments and delivery are real, but presumably resolvable. Smart software which can search out and order 'best buys' already exists or is in preparation.

The main problems for firms are likely to be logistical. Packing and delivering single items will be costly, especially if the recipient is out at the time of delivery. This opens the way for the fourth player – a parcel company, the Post Office, or newspaper distributor – to join the other three.

The cost implications of electronic shopping are as yet unclear. Providers would save store costs – perhaps 20 per cent of turnover – but would incur possibly higher technology and certainly delivery and marketing costs. Turnover would come under pressure as manufacturers tried to sell direct to the public on a lowest-price basis, although manufacturers would probably need to invest more than ever in branding.

The costs to the consumer, apart from the inconvenience associated with home delivery, would be those of time spent in search and in risk acceptance. In traditional retailing, the store's buyer presents the shopper with an edited range of goods, backed by its own quality guarantee. The store thus takes the front-line risk for faulty products.

Whichever way the balance of cost advantage finally works out, fixed site retailers of items currently sold through catalogues (clothing to watches to toys) and of branded basics (washing powders, canned goods) undoubtedly face a credible threat from a potential new entrant. Electronic shopping need take only a few sales percentage points to render marginal shops non-viable.

John Hollis of Andersen Consulting, which runs a demonstration 'Smart Store Europe' in Windsor for directors of manufacturers and retailers, predicts[36] that high streets are likely to lose 20 per cent of sales to home shopping by 2000. Should he be only half right, fixed-site retailers will be under pressure to diversify into electronic retailing.[37] This threat from the 'virtual shopping mall' will tend to force retailers to compete not just in terms of price, where they may or may not be vulnerable to electronic home shopping, but in terms of

---

[36] *Independent on Sunday*, 4 June 1995.

[37] Recently there have been rumours that Marks & Spencer has been considering a pre-emptive move: 'M & S considers mail order and electronic shopping', *The Guardian*, 24 July 1995.

reputation, range of products, exclusivity, ambience and customer services, where they are likely to be more secure.

Competition's Myriad Forms

The lesson which follows from this brief description of recent trends in UK retailing is a simple one, which analysts of retailing have known for many years but which deserves restating before public policy issues are considered. It is that, as Tucker and Yamey put it more than 20 years ago:

'The establishment of new types of retail operation is a major form in which competitive forces assert themselves in the market place.'[38]

Faced with apparently entrenched and successful players, new entrants to retailing have displayed enormous ingenuity in providing consumers with something different rather than merely copying existing practice; there is little sign of this ingenuity drying up. Such innovation may involve superior technology, but it may not. It may involve immense capital investment, but again it may not. What is important is the development of new ways of serving the customer. It is therefore worth emphasising that even apparently insignificant and unsophisticated retail activity can have a serious competitive impact on some existing retailers if it strikes a chord with the public.

Take, for instance, that seemingly ubiquitous phenomenon of the 1990s, the car boot sale. The British Retail Consortium has recently stigmatised such events (now running, incidentally, at anything up to 10,000 a year) as 'involving widespread illegal activity that represents unfair competition to the vast majority of law-abiding traders'.[39] It is true there is evidence that car boot sales feature video and audio piracy, resale of illegally imported alcoholic drink and cigarettes, and sale of stolen goods. However, the vast majority of traders and their customers are probably reasonably upright citizens who simply find it pleasurable or profitable to buy or sell a wide

---

[38] K.A. Tucker and B.S. Yamey (eds.), *The Economics of Retailing*, Penguin Modern Economics Readings, Harmondsworth: Penguin Books, 1973, Introduction, p.11.

[39] 'Car boot sales', *International Journal of Retail and Distribution Management*, Vol.4, 1994, p.ii.

range of old and new products in unlikely and sometimes aesthetically unappealing settings: we should be wary of allowing vested interests to dominate public policy towards brash newcomers.

Certainly the related phenomenon of street markets (which underwent a dramatic rejuvenation and revival in the 1970s and 1980s in areas such as London's Camden Lock and Petticoat Lane) offers an enjoyable and innovative shopping experience, with outlets for craft, ethnic and 'New Age' products which rarely find a home on the High Street. These markets also played a rôle in stimulating shopping hours reform by pioneering widespread Sunday trading, and provided major spin-offs to neighbourhood restaurants, pubs and entertainment facilities.

Any innovative opportunity for buyers and sellers to interact thus opens up possibilities for expanding consumer choice. While car boot sales are not most people's vision of the future of retailing, they are a reminder that competition takes many forms and often comes from the most unexpected quarters.

III. COMPETITION IN RETAILING

The preceding section indicated that UK retailing has altered dramatically in the last two decades, and is subject to continuing change as social conditions, tastes and technologies alter. But is this change always necessarily to the advantage of the consumer? Or do the benefits go disproportionately to the major firms which increasingly seem to dominate the market, while many smaller retailers and some consumers are losers? Do retailers, large and small, behave as if they were subject to constant competitive pressure to give their customers the best deal they can, or are they free to take and keep monopoly profits? And should governments intervene to assist the competitive process? This section explores some of the public policy issues associated with the competitive environment in retailing.

Market Structure and Competition

Since the beginning of systematic economic thinking, the need to maintain competition has been seen as a problem. At its simplest, this is shown in the textbook comparison between 'pure' monopoly and 'perfect' competition, which in modern guise dates back to the 1920s, and in cruder form to Adam Smith. It stresses the allocative inefficiency resulting from the power associated with one extreme of market structure, monopoly. In a tightly-specified (albeit highly unrealistic) model, a profit-maximising monopolist can be shown to produce a smaller output at a higher price than a competitive industry facing identical technological and demand parameters. Thus monopoly misallocates resources, a result which tyro economic students have long been expected to demonstrate.

The theoretical models of pure monopoly and perfect competition have often been criticised by such students (and many of their teachers) on the grounds that the assumptions[1]

---

[1] The perfectly competitive model, for example, assumes an indefinitely large number of buyers and sellers, perfect information, no entry barriers to or exit barriers from the market, and a single standardised product.

of these models are so restrictive as to exclude virtually all 'real world' markets – including the retail sector.

In the 1930s a more promising avenue seemed to be opened up by the theory of *monopolistic* (or *imperfect*) *competition* pioneered by Edward Chamberlin in the USA and Joan Robinson in the UK.[2] In this type of market structure many independent firms compete to sell products which are differentiated in some way from those of other firms. In retailing, for instance, different firms will offer a different mix of product range, location, customer service and so forth. This gives each firm a 'partial monopoly', in that consumers do not regard the output of other firms as a perfect substitute.

The monopolistic competition model suggests this differentiation is bought at a cost, for pursuit of profit maximisation produces an equilibrium where there exists excess capacity. The corollary is that goods are not produced and sold at the lowest technically possible price.[3] The consequences for consumer welfare are unclear; to the extent that consumers are willing to pay the cost of differentiation, they may be assumed to be better off doing so than they would be otherwise. To take a pertinent example, if a corner shop, because of its location, offers an everyday convenience which the hypermarket five miles away cannot offer, it may charge higher equilibrium prices (although still only making 'normal' profits). At prices as low as those of the hypermarket, it would go out of business and consumers would have to incur transport and time costs in travelling to the more distant store.

The theory of monopolistic competition, although superficially more realistic, is still an unconvincing picture of the world as we know it. The prediction of excess capacity in

[2] E.H. Chamberlin, *The Theory of Monopolistic Competition*, Cambridge, Mass.: Harvard University Press, 1933; J. Robinson, *The Economics of Imperfect Competition*, London: Macmillan, 1933.

[3] Because the consumer does not consider the firm's product a perfect substitute for other firms in the market, the demand curve for the firm's product (its average revenue curve) is downward sloping. However, in monopolistically competitive markets new firms can enter until supernormal profits are eliminated. This means that in equilibrium, average cost must equal average revenue as well as the familiar profit-maximising condition that *marginal* costs and revenue are equalised. These conditions are only met simultaneously when average costs are falling – that is, when firms are operating at less than full capacity.

equilibrium, though not implausible,[4] is derived as a result of dropping only one of the assumptions of perfect competition – product homogeneity. If we drop further assumptions – for instance, those of a large number of competing firms, and no barriers to entry – we move into the world of oligopoly. Here equilibrium price and output are indeterminate, as they depend on the reaction of firms to the behaviour of their competitors. Game theory – the branch of mathematics which examines the rational responses of players in situations of conflict and uncertainty – once promised to elucidate this issue. However, beyond elaborating and extending the concept of 'Nash equilibrium' (a situation where a firm makes the best possible response to the strategies of its rivals), it has created neither a useful model of firm behaviour nor simple and unambiguous policy conclusions.

Structure, Conduct and Performance

For many years economists and other analysts have tried to pursue less rigorous and more practical approaches to the question of market structure. One of the most influential of such approaches was developed by the *Harvard School* half a century ago. Recognising that in the real world there are no simple dichotomies between competition and monopoly, writers such as E.S. Mason and J.S. Bain[5] drew attention instead to the degree of concentration in an industry as a broad indicator of market power and hence of undesirable effects on economic welfare. This is the 'structure-conduct-performance' (SCP) paradigm.

---

[4] However, excess capacity in retailing is a problematic notion, given that shopping intensity varies throughout the day, week and year. For an early attempt to explore the implications of excess capacity in this sector see W.A. Lewis, 'Competition in Retail Trade', *Economica*, New Series, Vol.12, 1945, pp.202-34 (reproduced in K. A. Tucker and B.S. Yamey (eds.), *Economics of Retailing*, Penguin Modern Economics Readings, Harmondsworth: Penguin Books, 1973). Although Lewis believed excess capacity to be endemic in some parts of retailing, he saw no justification for government intervention to restrict the number of retailers.

[5] J.S. Bain, 'Relation of Profit Rate to Industrial Concentration: American Manufacturing 1936-40', *Quarterly Journal of Economics*, Vol.65, 1951, pp.293-324, and *Barriers to New Competition*, Cambridge, Mass.: Harvard University Press, 1956; E.S. Mason, 'Price and Production Policies of Large Scale Enterprises', *American Economic Review*, Supplement to Vol.29, 1939, pp.61-74.

Here basic market conditions (elasticities of demand, technology, and so on) determine *structure* (as evidenced by market concentration and associated barriers to entry),[6] which in turn affects *conduct* (for example, pricing strategies and anti-competitive practices); finally conduct determines *performance* (for example, profitability, growth and efficiency). This appears to present a testable hypothesis. In extreme versions of the SCP model, detailed examination of conduct is unnecessary, for structure *requires* certain types of conduct, which then leads directly to performance. To test the hypothesis we can take, for example, measures of market concentration and examine their relationship to indicators of performance such as profitability.

If the expected relationships are found,[7] there seem to be clear implications for competition policy: the approach has been used to justify vigorous anti-trust action in the United States. The Harvard School, together with its more recent derivative the *Structuralist* School, has historically been associated with strong support for the *per se* doctrine, an important feature of the American anti-trust legal tradition. This doctrine holds market dominance to be harmful in itself; it should therefore be illegal. By contrast, in the more pragmatic 'cost-benefit' tradition of the UK, the Monopolies and Mergers Commission is often required to weigh the disadvantages of market power against possible compensating advantages (for example, scale economies passed on to the consumer in lower prices). However, some version of the SCP argument also underlies the UK emphasis on the proportion of the market (25 per cent) controlled by one supplier as a

---

[6] There are alternative definitions of a 'barrier to entry'. For Bain this means anything which places potential entrants at a disadvantage compared with established firms, thus enabling 'supernormal' profits to be maintained over time by incumbents. Bain referred to *absolute cost* (patents, lower-cost finance), *economies of scale* and *product differentiation* as the main types of entry barriers.

[7] Evidence on the supposed relationship between market concentration and industry-average profitability is, however, underwhelming. Cross-sectional studies until the early 1970s seemed to indicate the existence of a weak positive correlation. However, since then, more sophisticated industry-level studies in the US and the UK have led to the conclusion that such a correlation does not generally exist. (See, for example, P.E. Hart and R. Clarke, *Concentration in British Industry 1935-1975*, Cambridge: Cambridge University Press, 1980.)

criterion for referral to the Monopolies and Mergers Commission.

Concentration in UK Retailing

As explained in Section II – and illustrated more fully in Table 6 – UK retailing as a whole exhibits growing concentration. In parts of the sector, notably food retailing, concentration is much higher than the average across the sector. Moreover, concentration in food retailing, at least, appears somewhat higher than in comparable European countries: data for the UK, France and Germany are shown in Table 7.

Although the evidence is open to different interpretations, over the 1980s gross retail margins in the UK seem to have risen broadly in line with this increasing concentration, as Figure 2 illustrates.

As for profitability, the evidence suggests that profit margins, although naturally varying over the business cycle, are higher in the UK than in most other European countries. For example, Table 8 shows that in 1992 eight out of Europe's 10 most profitable retailers were British.

Does it follow, then, that the UK's increasingly concentrated retailing sector has meant reduced competition, enabling the leading firms to obtain exceptionally high profits at consumers' expense? This is much more difficult to establish.

Take the evidence of gross margins. Although a rise in gross margins *may* reflect an increase in market power, there are other possible explanations. One is that high margins are largely a consequence of the very high level of investment in retailing in recent years: throughout the 1980s and the early 1990s, retailing's share of UK investment significantly exceeded its share of GDP. This extra investment had, of course, to be paid for. A recent study of grocery retailing by the consultancy London Economics[8] shows that, for 15 leading grocery retailers (accounting for 65 per cent of total grocery sales), turnover tripled between 1984 and 1992 but capital costs rose by a factor of five.

However, Table 9 shows that increasing margins in retailing are not confined to those big players (and heaviest investors) whose market dominance might seem to have been enhanced over time. This is particularly clear in the case of food retailing,

[*continued on page 42*]

---

[8] London Economics, *The Grocery Retailing Revolution,* June 1995.

TABLE 6:
Proportion of Retail Sales Accounted for by
Five Largest Enterprise Groups: UK, 1982-93

1982	0·14
1984	0·16
1986	0·18
1988	0·19
1990	0·20
1991	0·21
1993	0·23

Source: Business Monitor

TABLE 7:
Market Share of Top Four Food Retailers:
France, Germany and the UK, 1982-90

	France	Germany	UK
1982	na	28·0	38·1
1988	33·2	36·5	51·6
1990	47·3	46·2	53·6

Source: L. Zanderighi and E. Zaninotto, 'Property rights distribution in European retailing', *The International Review of Retail Distribution and Consumer Research*, Vol. 4, No. 4, 1994.

TABLE 8:
Europe's Top Retailers: by pre-tax profit margin, 1992

Company	Home Country	Profit Margin %
Great Universal Stores	Britain	16·9
Marks & Spencer	Britain	12·4
Benetton	Italy	11·3
Boots	Britain	10·2
Argyll	Britain	8·0
Tesco	Britain	7·7
J. Sainsbury	Britain	7·6
El Corte Ingles	Spain	7·4
Wm. Morrison	Britain	6·4
Kingfisher	Britain	5·8

Source: The Economist, 4 March 1995.

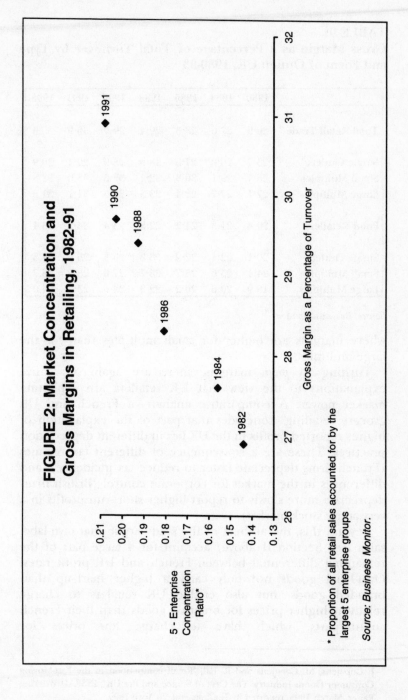

FIGURE 2: Market Concentration and Gross Margins in Retailing, 1982-91

Source: Business Monitor.

* Proportion of all retail sales accounted for by the largest 5 enterprise groups

5 - Enterprise Concentration Ratio*

Gross Margin as a Percentage of Turnover

TABLE 9:
Gross Margin as a Percentage of Total Turnover by Type and Form of Outlet: UK, 1980-93

	1980	1984	1986	1988	1990	1991	1993
Total Retail Trade	26·9	27·6	28·3	29·4	29·7	30·9	30.3
Single Outlets	25·7	26·9	27·3	28·5	28·9	29·4	30.9
Small Multiples	28·7	29·1	30·3	32·2	32·6	33·0	32.8
Large Multiples	27·1	27·7	28·4	29·3	29·5	31·1	31.8
Food Retailers	20·4	21·3	21·2	22·8	23·4	24·2	23.4
Single Outlets	20·1	22·1	22·9	23·3	25·3	25·9	21.3
Small Multiples	24·1	25·6	25·7	26·7	27·6	28·5	26.7
Large Multiples	19·9	20·6	20·2	22·3	22·6	23·5	24.0

Source: Business Monitor.

where margins are higher for small multiples than for the large multiples.

Turning to *profit* margins, there are again alternative explanations to the view that UK retailers are exploiting market power. A comparative analysis of French and UK grocery retailing[9] concludes that part of the explanation of higher reported profits in the UK lies in different depreciation practices. These are a consequence of different tax régimes (French firms depreciate faster to reduce tax incidence), and differences in the market for corporate control (British firms depreciate more slowly to report higher short-run profits in a very active stock market).

Beyond this, the authors of the study argue that own-label sales (see Section II above) account for a large part of the remaining differential between French and UK profit rates. Own-label goods not only carry a higher mark-up than branded goods, but also enable UK retailers to charge relatively higher prices for branded goods than their French counterparts, which have to charge low prices for

---

[9] J. Corstjens, M. Corstjens and R. Lal, 'Retail competition in the Fast-Moving Consumer Goods Industry: The Case of France and the UK', INSEAD Working Paper, March 1995, reported in *The Economist*, 29 April 1995.

manufacturers' brands to attract customers. The major French grocery retailers find it difficult to emulate the British majors' own-label strategy because of legal restrictions on television advertising in deference to France's small shopkeeper lobby.

Other analysts, such as London Economics, have explained high profits in grocery retailing by reference to specific advantages achieved by the leading players as a result of the innovative use of new technology, as described earlier, and the provision of innovative services to the consumer. It certainly appears that the most successful retailers add considerable value, which is naturally reflected in the prices charged and profits obtained. In 1989, Sainsbury's advantage over Asda (then the weakest of the major superstore operators) was 10 per cent, implying that a unit of net output cost Sainsbury's only 90 per cent of what it cost Asda. According to Professor John Kay, the author of the calculation,

> 'This is a measure of the difference in value created by a highly successful firm, with strong distinctive capabilities, over that achieved by the merely competent'.[10]

How Important are Barriers to Entry?

Such supernormal profits can persist over time for two reasons. One is that the leading players may be constantly innovating successfully in order to stay ahead. The other is that there may be significant barriers to entry. How important are such barriers in UK retailing? Consider:

- Unlike in many other countries, there are no significant barriers to foreign firms, which can and do enter freely.[11]

- Economies of scale and scope, outlined in the previous section, may appear to suggest new entry entails prohibitive capital outlay. However, the capital required in retailing, though substantial, is not particularly large compared with

---

[10] John Kay, *Foundations of Corporate Success*, Oxford University Press, 1993, pp.193-95.

[11] For example, American retailers have entered the UK market to a much greater extent than the markets of most other European countries. (*Source:* Corporate Intelligence, *Cross-Border Retailing in Europe*, London: Corporate Intelligence Research Publications, 1995.)

many manufacturing processes (plant) or financial services (reserve funds) where entry is common.

- In any case, there are ways round any such problem. For example, independent retailers can combine their buying power through symbol groups (for example, Spar and VG) or other co-operative ventures, such as the National Independent Supermarkets Association (NISA), which, with £9 billion turnover, is currently one of the largest grocery buying points in the country.[12]

- The use of electronic cost-saving technologies (Section II above) does not necessarily imply large-scale operations, particularly if customised software can be used.

- Minimum efficient store size depends on the market being served and the mode of store operation. Discounters typically operate with between 500 and 1,000 lines, against the superstores' 15,000 to 20,000. Narrow aisles and few frills are far less space-hungry than a state-of-the-art grocery superstore and may suit a particularly price-conscious clientele.

- Small retailers may even have some advantages over their larger rivals, in terms of rapid response to changes in local demand, whereas national chains, with their centralised controls, can sometimes leave little or no scope to their local managers for instant initiatives.

- Professionally crafted national reputations can give the major chains an advantage in terms of customer and local government relations. However real local relationships, based on personal contacts, can often prove more durable than those managed from head office. The survival of the independent sector depends on entrepreneurship and innovation, a willingness to work longer hours for lower margins, than is the case in the multiple chains. As Box 1 illustrates, their strength is to offer something different in a world in which the majors imitate each other's moves.

---

[12] *Consortium*, Issue 11, 1994; NISA services independent grocers with turnover in excess of £2 million, wholesalers and the Londis and Cost Cutter groups.

BOX 1

Jempsons of Peasmarsh – A Case Study in Doing it Differently

Winner of the Independent Grocer of the Year award for 1994, Jempsons of Peasmarsh, Sussex, provides a remarkable example of an independent grocer able to compete against the national grocery chains. Peasmarsh is a small rural village of some 400 houses, within easy driving distance from supermarkets and superstores in nearby Hastings, Tenterden, Ashford and Rye.

Jempsons, founded as a bakery in 1935 and still family-managed, carries over 22,000 different product lines, larger than the typical superstore, in 12,000 square feet – perhaps half the size of their rivals. It operates a petrol station, with a car wash and parking for 120 cars, and a Post Office – these had previously proved uneconomic in so small a village. The store also runs its own café, butchery, bakery, fishmongers, confectioners and delicatessen (which, for example, sells a range of more than 100 cheeses).

The *Independent Grocer* said that the Jempsons store 'defied all logic in that it prospered in an area which by all the usual criteria could scarcely support a local store'.

The store runs its own free weekday bus service bringing in shoppers from a 12-mile radius. The store claims to attract shoppers from as far afield as Tunbridge Wells – a major shopping centre 20 miles away. This bus service ties in the store to its catchment area and is particularly valued by pensioner customers, who turn shopping into a weekly outing. When the Post Office closed in Rye Harbour, five miles away, pensioners were offered a choice of collecting their pensions in nearby Rye or travelling on the free bus to collect them in the Peasmarsh store. The Jempson name is locally well established, given the 60 years over which the firm has baked and supplied bread to the district – it even runs a bread and tea shop in Rye.

Jempsons is a member of NISA, which enables it to compete on range and price with the national chains, although the independent sector as a whole may have a reputation with the shopping public for high prices and narrow ranges. In addition to the lines purchased from NISA, Jempsons is able to stock local produce, including locally caught sea fish, so providing an individuality lacking in the majors. Its ingenious use of space adds to the store's relaxed character, as do the friendly staff, who mainly live locally.

In 1982 it was one of the first two independent grocers to introduce computerised scanning, ahead of many of the majors. This provides a level of inventory management which matches that of the national chains. However, Jempsons relies far more on local judgement than on computerised sales forecasts for buying decisions.

Sources: 'Award Winners in the Limelight: the best in the business!', *Independent Grocer*, 14 October 1994; personal interview.

It seems unlikely that barriers to entry associated with minimum efficient size are any greater in the UK than in other European countries. Nor does it seem that artificial barriers to entry associated with government regulation are greater here than elsewhere in Europe. There was substantial planning deregulation in Britain in the 1980s (although this has to some extent been reversed more recently), and shop opening hours have been greatly liberalised in the UK while considerable restrictions still exist in, for example, Germany and France.

One possible disadvantage which potential entrants to retailing face in the UK to a greater extent than elsewhere is the cost and availability of property. Rents and property taxes in London's main shopping areas are higher than in any other major European city,[13] while the cost of land for out-of-town developments is also much higher than in many other countries. Moreover, John Burton has argued that the peculiar British system of long-term property leases with 'upward-only' rent revisions creates an incentive for landlords to leave valuable high street sites empty rather than lower rents.[14] This penalises small businesses and, by reducing the supply of affordable premises, deters new entry. More will be said about this issue in Section IV.

On the whole, however, the persistence of high profits in retailing seems unlikely to be the product of barriers to entry.

Other Approaches to Competition

The Chicago School v. Harvard/Structuralist School

The Structuralist view of the evils of concentration and the significance of entry barriers has not had the academic field to itself. Throughout the post-war period there has been a strong rival tradition in the form of the Chicago School. Chicago economists, most notably the late George Stigler,[15] take exception to the view that concentrated markets are dangerous in themselves. Emphasis is placed instead on the benefits of economies of scale and other efficiency gains accruing to large

---

[13] 'Change at the check-out', *The Economist*, 4 March 1995, p.13.

[14] John Burton, *Retail Rents: Fair and Free Market?*, London: Adam Smith Institute, 1992.

[15] G.J. Stigler, *The Organisation of Industry*, Homewood, Illinois: R.D. Irwin, 1968.

firms. In any case, the strong belief in market forces associated with Chicago economics leads these researchers to claim that the entry barriers emphasised by the Harvard and Structuralist schools are more apparent than real.[16] In the long run, competition is sufficiently powerful to undermine attempts by firms to rig markets. If supernormal profits persist for any length of time it is likely to be because entrepreneurs possess unique skills or other resources which command an economic rent or scarcity payment.[17]

Two examples serve to illustrate the differences between the schools. First, take the well-known practice of *vertical integration* (where firms attempt to control a number of different production stages between the extraction of raw materials and the sale to the public of finished products). Whereas the Harvard/Structuralist writers see this practice as anti-competitive, Chicago authors have argued forcefully that it does not threaten consumer welfare. They claim that, even if a particular industry is characterised by monopoly at all stages of production, there is no reason why entry should not occur. Profitable opportunities exist which should attract capital and new entry. Entry would probably have to be by other vertically-integrated concerns, but such entry should be forthcoming unless there are capital market imperfections. If no entry occurs, and supernormal profits persist, the capital market cannot be working correctly – but it will be this, rather than vertical integration, which is the problem.

Chicago economists point out that vertical integration can bring positive benefits to the consumer in the form of lower costs, and should not be seen as a threat to competition. Vertical integration in retailing, incidentally, has a mixed

---

[16] C.f. Stigler's alternative definition of a barrier to entry as 'a cost of producing...which must be borne by a firm which seeks to enter an industry but is not borne by firms already in the industry' (Stigler, *ibid.*, p.67). In this view product differentiation (an example of Bain's barriers to entry) through extensive advertising is *not* a genuine entry barrier – incumbents will also have had to incur the costs of entry themselves in the past. Many of Bain's barriers turn out simply to reflect the date of a firm's entry and are more accurately described as *first mover advantage*. (See P.R. Ferguson and G.J. Ferguson, *Industrial Economics: Issues and Perspectives*, London and Basingstoke: Macmillan, 2nd edn., 1994, p.20.)

[17] See H. Demsetz, 'Industry Structure, Market Rivalry, and Public Policy', *Journal of Law and Economics*, Vol.16, 1973, pp.1-9.

history. Emphasis in the UK is currently on separating manufacturing from retailing. The Co-operative Wholesale Society has recently been disinvesting upstream, in order to concentrate on its core business. The brewers are (albeit reluctantly) developing separate manufacturing and retail arms.

A second, and very pertinent, example is the case of *exclusive dealing* (a contractual arrangement whereby retailers or distributors promise a supplier not to handle competing products).[18] Such contracts obviously protect suppliers; the benefit to retailers is usually in the form of a franchise to be the sole outlet in a particular area. Harvard/Structuralist writers see potential harm to consumers in the form of higher prices, and condemn such arrangements as anti-competitive.

Chicago economists, however, have argued it is legitimate for suppliers to seek exclusive dealerships in compensation for their investment in advertising and sales promotion. Without exclusive dealership, retailers could 'free ride' on promotional investment. With it, producers find it worthwhile to enter new markets and develop new products. Exclusive dealing can thus, paradoxically, promote competition indirectly.

This position remains a controversial one. The recent case involving perfume manufacturers' refusal to supply High Street retailers Superdrug (discussed later in this section) illustrates the problems raised by pushing this argument to its logical extreme. It has, nevertheless, had a considerable impact on thinking about competition policy.

The Austrians

In recent years, the attack on the structure-conduct-performance paradigm has been joined by a resurgence in 'Austrian' approaches to competition: ideas inspired by such writers as Carl Menger, Ludwig von Mises, Joseph Schumpeter and Friedrich Hayek. Austrians have always been associated

---

[18] An interesting recent development is discussion of the issue of vertical integration in the context of the 'new institutional economics', where the form of economic organisation – and in particular, the ever-shifting boundaries between exchange in a market and production within a firm – is strongly influenced by the nature and extent of transactions costs. In this context, exclusive dealing and similar practices are substitutes for vertical integration. (See O.E. Williamson, *The Economic Institutions of Capitalism*, New York: Free Press, 1985.)

with a robustly free-market stance, and perhaps even more strongly with an abhorrence of government involvement in the economy. Thus they tend to play down the need for government intervention to prevent market concentration.

Neo-Austrians[19] are sceptical of the existence of long-run market power, and certainly of the link between market concentration and market power postulated by the Harvard School. They believe that, if there are no legal barriers to entry, a high level of concentration in a particular market merely reflects underlying cost conditions. Indeed, virtually no genuine economic entry barriers are believed to exist.

According to neo-Austrians, persistent examples of the abuse of market power by producers tend to arise only where enterprises are protected from competition by the state – for example, nationalised industries. By contrast, firms in a genuinely free market are unable to maintain supernormal profits for very long, as such profits attract new entrants. These may not (and this is a crucial point) be producers of identical products, but rather products in a related field. Thus conventional measures of market concentration may remain unchanged, but the boundaries of the 'real' market may shift. Word processors compete with typewriters, spicy corn chips with potato crisps, video games with board games, home shopping with department stores.

So neo-Austrians worry little about market concentration if free entry is feasible. Supernormal profits are seen as temporary, and a necessary spur to competition. Government intervention may actually make markets work less well. For instance, price or profit controls on regulated industries reduce the attractiveness of new entry and thus paradoxically protect the position of incumbents. Firms contemplating innovation and invention may be deterred if the profits they can make are threatened by state regulators. As leading British neo-Austrian Stephen Littlechild has argued,[20] it is all very well complaining about the high price of a product if the alternative is a lower price under competition, but if the alternative

---

[19] For an introduction to neo-Austrian thinking see S.C. Littlechild, *The Fallacy of the Mixed Economy*, Hobart Paper No.80, London: Institute of Economic Affairs, 1978, Second Edition, 1986.

[20] S.C. Littlechild, 'Misleading Calculations of the Social Costs of Monopoly Power', *Economic Journal*, Vol.91, 1981, pp.348-63.

is that no product is available because nobody has an incentive to invent it, things look different.

The relevance for retailing is that neo-Austrians reject the idea that supernormal profits in retailing, if they exist, are more than a transient phenomenon, a reward for temporary superiority in a market continually being reconfigured by innovation. They would not see such profits as indicating a need for government intervention.

Contestable Markets

Another influential view of the market power issue is the 'contestable market' approach initiated by the American economist, William J. Baumol.[21] In Baumol's view, also, economists have been wrong to worry too much about market concentration: the number of firms in an industry at a particular moment is irrelevant if they are free to enter and (very importantly) leave the market without making substantial losses. Such freedom of entry and exit makes possible a 'hit-and-run' competitive strategy. Firms enter when producers are making supernormal profits, and leave as soon as those profits disappear. This is only possible in the absence of *sunk costs* (that is, those which cannot be recouped on leaving the industry). Sunk costs, which should be distinguished from the fixed costs (those which do not vary with output changes) of standard neo-classical theory, are those which arise from investing in specific assets which have little or no value in other uses.

A market where sunk costs are low, where investment in specific assets is minimal (as seems likely to be the case in much of retailing),[22] is what Baumol means by a contestable market. In such a case, *even if there are only one or two currently active suppliers*, supernormal profits cannot persist. Were they to do so, new firms would enter and compete away the excess. As existing firms are assumed to be aware of this, they will refrain from exploiting their apparent market power even in the absence of new entrants. The implication is that one should beware of assuming that the existence of high

---

[21] W.J. Baumol, 'Contestable Markets: An Uprising in the Theory of Industrial Structure', *American Economic Review*, Vol.72, 1982, pp.1-15.

[22] Premises can be leased out, unsold stock sold at bargain prices. What may, however, have to be written off is investment in reputation.

concentration in retailing is necessarily associated with abnormally high profits or other indicators of market power.[23]

Anti-Competitive Practices

The apparent weakening of the case against market concentration *per se* has led many economists – and government competition and regulatory agencies – to look at firms' conduct rather than at market structure.

Consequently in the UK, particularly since the 1980 Competition Act, the focus of competition policy has often been on *restrictive* or *anti-competitive practices* – means by which a firm or firms seek to restrict or prevent competition. Such means include resale price maintenance, exclusive dealing, predatory pricing, discounting, tied sales and franchising. Government action to outlaw these practices implies acceptance of something like the 'structure-conduct-performance' model, for it assumes that the erection of entry barriers can have the lasting effect of boosting a firm's profits. But, given the doubts about the SCP paradigm expressed by Chicagoans, Austrians and others, it is not surprising that there are differences of opinion about the desirability of government action. Here we briefly review two forms of anti-competitive practice.

Resale Price Maintenance

In the UK most attention in the 1950s and 1960s centred on resale price maintenance (RPM) – the practice by which manufacturers (either collectively or individually) refuse to supply their products to retailers unless the latter agree to resell them to the public at a fixed price. The effect is to reduce or even eliminate price competition and thus artificially maintain a larger number of smaller retailers in existence than would otherwise be the case. Christina Fulop (following the lead of B. S. Yamey in the first *Hobart Paper*[24]) took a strong line in favour of abolishing RPM; it was duly

---

[23] All these arguments tend to be based on theoretical rather than empirical grounds. For a piece of empirical work which attempts to test the implications of some of these ideas and comes to a rather negative view, see R. W. Cotterill and L. E. Haller, 'Barrier and Queue Effects: A Study of Leading US Supermarket Chain Entry Patterns', *Journal of Industrial Economics*, Vol.XL, December 1992, pp.427-40.

[24] B.S. Yamey, *Resale Price Maintenance and Shoppers' Choice*, Hobart Paper No.1, 1960, Fourth Edition 1964.

proscribed by the Resale Prices Act of 1964. The Act provided for exemption in cases where abandonment of RPM could convincingly be argued to reduce consumer welfare (by increasing retail prices, reducing the quality or variety of goods or the number of retail outlets, allowing goods to be sold under conditions dangerous to health or reducing necessary after-sales service); however, in only two cases, pharmaceuticals and books, have defences succeeded in squeezing through these 'gateways'.

In the book trade, the Net Book Agreement (NBA) until recently meant that a particular book was sold at the same price in all UK outlets. The result has been that the structure of book retailing in this country remains quite unlike that of most other retailing sectors – and very different from countries such as the USA where no such agreement exists. For instance, multiples account for only 35 per cent of book sales, in contrast to 80 per cent of grocery sales.[25] Restrictions on price competition led to a rise in the relative price of books and proliferation of new titles as publishers competed for market share, while Book Clubs (selling special cheap editions of popular titles) grew up to take a significant share of the market. The justification for RPM in the book trade was that it enabled smaller stores to continue stocking large ranges of books. Arguably, however, it discouraged innovation in bookselling.[26] Whatever the final verdict, the NBA has now collapsed as a result of major publishers deciding it was no longer in their interests.[27]

The firmness of UK law on RPM is not found everywhere. European Union law is more ambiguous. Individual RPM is permitted, so long as retailers are free to buy from any supplier by parallel imports. The USA presents the most interesting case. Here, despite the *per se* bias of American anti-

---

[25] See G. Warnaby and J. Upton, 'Are Books Different? The Impact of Price on Retail Market Development?', *International Journal of Retail and Distribution Management*, Vol.22, No.4, pp.13-19.

[26] W. Allan and P. Curwen, *Competition and Choice in the Publishing Industry*, Hobart Paper No.116, London: Institute of Economic Affairs, 1991.

[27] In September 1995 HarperCollins, Penguin and Random House announced that they were withdrawing from the NBA, following the earlier lead of Reed and Hodder Headline. This led the Publishers Association to announce that it would no longer help enforce the agreement.

trust law, RPM has been in and out of favour. In 1911 it was ruled to be a violation of the Sherman Act; it was then, however, legalised. In the mid-1970s, however, 'fair trade' legislation permitting RPM was repealed and the original prohibition restored. By the 1980s the position had changed again and, like many other forms of vertical restraint in the aftermath of the *Sylvania* judgement of 1977 in the US Supreme Court,[28] RPM was no longer challenged.

Resale price maintenance is no longer a major issue in the UK, although related forms of refusal to supply (see Box 2) still surface from time to time. The recent changes in theoretical perspective described above, coupled with Britain's changed relationship with Europe, may suggest greater ambivalence towards RPM than at the time of the 1964 Act, when market economists generally took a critical view. In a Chicago or neo-Austrian framework, for example, it is possible to defend the practice. It is difficult to see any significant constituency for a reversal of UK policy and the restoration of RPM in its pre-1964 form. However, a strongly pro-market government could permit RPM to emerge as the result of market processes for individual products.

Manufacturer Price Discounting

Small shopkeepers often supported RPM prior to the 1964 Act, believing it worked in their interest. In the 1980s attention shifted to another aspect of the relation between manufacturers and retailers – the practice of differential price discounting by manufacturers. Large retailers, particularly in the grocery trade, were able to negotiate substantial reductions in the prices they paid manufacturers for goods. Small shopkeepers and the smaller multiples predictably saw this as unfair competition, an echo of the arguments about RPM.

Retailing was investigated by the competition authorities twice in the decade; in neither case did their conclusions lead them to take action against the industry. In 1981 the Monopolies and Mergers Commission[29] reported on three years of

[*continued on page 56*]

---

[28] Discussed in Terry Burke, Angela Genn-Bash and Brian Haines, *Competition in Theory and Practice*, London: Routledge, 1991, p.142

[29] MMC, *Discounts to Retailers*, House of Commons 311.

BOX 2

The Ghost of RPM: Perfumes and Jeans

Resale Price Maintenance may be outlawed in the UK, but related phenomena remain.

An intriguing battle has been taking place between Superdrug and Boots for the fragrance market, with Superdrug playing the part of the challenger.

Superdrug, a mature (30 years' experience) and substantial (670 stores) business, has for the past five years been trying to change the balance of its product mix away from reliance on core toiletries (soaps, shampoos, toothpaste, and so on), the sales of which have substantially moved to the grocery superstores, to a greater emphasis on fragrances.

There is a large UK market for fragrances (perfumes, aftershave and related products): sales were in excess of £500 million in 1994. These products are highly priced (up to 60 per cent mark-up), highly promoted (in excess of £100 million annual advertising[1]) and offer packaged 'dreams in a bottle': they give customers a whiff of glamorous and exotic lifestyles.

Superdrug believes that the profit margins enjoyed by Boots, the leading high street perfume retailer, are too high. The company believes it can offer fragrances in its stores at roughly the same prices as those found in duty-free outlets on cross-Channel ferries and in airports – that is, around a quarter to a third cheaper than in a Boots store where there is no local competitor.

Superdrug believes that lower prices will not only win it a substantial share, but will expand the market overall. It argues that for perfumes, as for almost all other known goods, demand curves slope downwards. It has, however, been frustrated by a refusal on the part of the perfume houses to supply through the normal channels. Instead, Superdrug has been buying a limited quantity of fragrances through the 'grey' market, in which authorised wholesalers and retailers offer their legitimately-purchased surplus stock for sale.

---

1 Industry sources.

The perfume manufacturers do not wish to supply Superdrug because they believe that price cutting will damage the whole market. They argue that fragrance products are sold overwhelmingly on the premise of exclusivity – their attraction is inseparably associated with their high price. Consumers use price as an indicator of desirability.

The suppliers therefore claim that they, and their chosen retailers, have invested heavily in the exclusive presentation of the product and have a right to exclude free-riders, who exploit the demand for perfume through price without contributing to the quality image.

The European Union (under Article 85 exemptions) accepts that perfume manufacturers can refuse to supply on objective grounds of quality of outlet (premises, staff, displays), but not, of course, on grounds of price.

Perhaps a clearer-cut case concerns jeans. Levi Strauss has recently withdrawn its jeans from Matalan, a chain of members-only discount warehouses with 50 outlets. Matalan's chairman, John Hargreaves, is quoted as saying: 'We do not feel it is appropriate that powerful suppliers should dictate in this way to our customers.'

Matalan, which has taken the matter to the Office of Fair Trading, offers members own label clothing at a discount of between 25 and 50 per cent and sells Levi 501 Jeans for £35 compared with a normal department store price of £45.

Levi Strauss rejects accusations that it is operating a back-door retail price maintenance policy. Its refusal to supply, it says, is based on Matalan's restrictive membership policy.

A Levi Strauss spokesman is quoted as saying: 'We sell jeans to retailers at a wholesale price and they are free to set their own price. There is not a manufacturer's recommended price.'

Whatever the particular long-term outcome of the Matalan complaint or of Superdrug's desire to sell perfumes, these cases suggest that there is still an area for dispute over refusal to supply. Some would no doubt argue (despite recent radical critiques of competition policy) that they suggest a plausible case for a continuing role for regulation.

---

2 'Levi's ban gives cost cutters the blues', *Daily Mail*, 2 June 1995.

years of study of the practice of discounting which had been claimed by its critics to involve an unacceptable use of market power by large multiple retailers. It was held 'to damage manufacturers' profits and to put smaller traders at a disadvantage so they cannot compete'.[30]

For 12 selected manufacturers, the MMC investigation found that the cost of special terms offered to larger retailers was 6·6 per cent of the value of total sales; for the top four retailers it was 9·2 per cent. Big volume manufacturers, such as bakers, complained that such pressure on their profits hit investment and research, while small retailers complained of loss of market share. The first complaint was downplayed; while it was accepted that the latter had some substance, it was felt that this was offset by gains to the consumer in terms of lower prices, for on the whole the discount was passed on in lower retail prices charged by the big multiples. A similarly permissive view was taken by the Office of Fair Trading in its 1985 report, *Competition and Retailing*: no action was required because there was strong competition.

In reaching their verdicts, the competition authorities were probably aware that, even if the findings had been against the big retailers, such findings would have been difficult to enforce. Where legal control of manufacturers' discounts has been attempted 'it has proved difficult and costly to enforce and is frequently circumvented – for example, by an increase in special formulations [i.e. own label goods] for each major retailer'.[31] Although they raise prices to the consumer, controls on discounts are therefore unlikely in the long run to preserve the market share of smaller retailers.

Local Monopolies?

The enforceability of competition laws is an issue which critics of UK competition policy do not always consider sufficiently. The authors of a recent Institute for Public Policy Research (IPPR) paper[32] have attracted attention with their complaint

---

[30] J. Bamfield, 'Competition and Change in British Retailing', *National Westminster Bank Quarterly Review*, February 1988, p.26.

[31] J. Bamfield, *ibid.*, p.27.

[32] Hugh Raven and Tim Lang with Caroline Dumonteil, *Off our Trolleys? Food retailing and the hypermarket economy*, London: Institute for Public Policy Research, 1995.

that the Monopoly and Mergers Commission's powers to investigate markets where a firm or complex of firms controls 25 per cent of UK sales are wrongly specified: in their view these powers should relate, in the case of grocery retailing, to *local* markets.[33]

This proposal is difficult to take seriously. Developments in grocery retailing in the last 20 years have almost certainly increased rather than reduced competition at the local level, as the large multiples are now national rather than regional players. In any case, it is difficult to see how the proposal could be put into effect. Local markets are very difficult to define unambiguously: travel-to-shop distances are not fixed, but depend on price differentials in relation to transport costs (many Norwegians do their Christmas shopping at Gateshead's Metro Centre!).

Moreover, the existence of the new forms of distance shopping discussed earlier, warehouse clubs and so on further complicates the picture for many products. Even granted a generally accepted definition, the task competition regulators would face with such a policy is potentially enormous, and offers limited benefits. Even if superstores are dominant in local markets, it is likely to be at least in part a result of their being able to sell at low prices because of their strong position in relation to suppliers. Regulation which dealt with this at the local level would be likely to reach the same conclusion the MMC has reached at the national level. As the benefits of lower supply prices tend to be passed on to the consumer in one way or another, it is difficult to see what type of intervention would be justified or, equally important, acceptable to local superstore shoppers.

Aggregate Cost Savings to Consumers

To conclude this section: UK retailing may be highly concentrated, but no convincing case has been made that this concentration is harmful to the public interest. Recent theoretical developments suggest that a high degree of concentration need imply nothing about the extent of competition in practice. As explained in Section II, competition takes many forms in the retail sector. There is no

---

[33] 'The geographical definition of a market in retail competition policy should be re-drawn on a consumers' travel-to-shop basis.' (Raven *et al.*, *ibid.*, p.51.)

reason to suppose the sector will be any less competitive in the future than it was in the past.

The most heavily concentrated sector is food retailing, yet that is where change continues to be most dramatic and competitive innovation most apparent. Although that alone is not conclusive evidence of the reality of competition and its benefits to the consumer, it is worth observing, as Figure 3 illustrates, that in recent years increases in food prices have consistently been less than increases in prices in general.

A more systematic analysis of the price impact of productivity gains associated with changes in the structure of grocery retailing over the period 1984-92 was conducted by London Economics. Using its Grocery Retail Model, it found that the improved performance of the 15 leading grocery retailers was in large measure passed on to consumers in the form of lower prices. Consumers benefited by a total of £4·2 billion in 1992, while the gain to shareholders was £95 million. The results indicate that the average weekly saving in the household's grocery bill amounted to £3·50. Of this, it is estimated that 75p was the result of efficiency improvements and £2·75 the result of passing on reduced input prices.[34] There is little support here for the view that large grocery retailers act uncompetitively.

---

[34] London Economics, *The Grocery Retailing Revolution*, op.cit., pp.25-29.

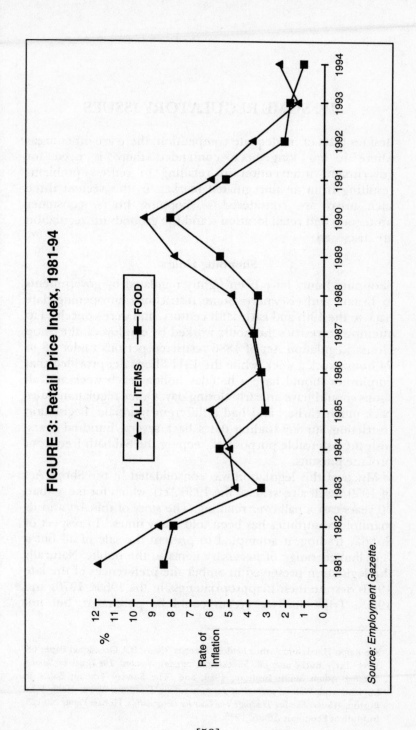

FIGURE 3: Retail Price Index, 1981-94

Rate of
Inflation

%

ALL ITEMS   FOOD

1981 1982 1983 1984 1985 1986 1987 1988 1989 1990 1991 1992 1993 1994

Source: Employment Gazette.

IV. SOME REGULATORY ISSUES

Besides fears of inadequate competition, there are other areas where it has long been contended there is need for government intervention in retailing to redress problems resulting from an unregulated market. In this section three such areas are considered – shopping hours, consumer protection and retail location – and the grounds for regulation are discussed.

Shopping Hours

Shopping hours have been tightly regulated by governments in Britain and elsewhere. Some restrictions on opening date back to the 19th and early 20th century, and were conceived as attempts to restrict the hours worked by employees: the Shop Hours Regulation Act of 1886 restricted persons under 18 to 74 hours work a week, while the 1911 Shops Act provided that employees should have a half-day holiday each week and all shops should have an early closing day. Other regulation dates back much earlier, and had a different rationale. Legislation restricting Sunday trading dates back several hundred years, with the ostensible purpose of keeping the Sabbath free from profane pursuits.

Much of this legislation was consolidated in the Shops Act of 1950 (itself a re-write of the 1936 Act), which for more than 40 years cast a pall over retailing. The story of this Act and its manifold absurdities has been told many times.[1] In respect of Sunday trading, it attempted to prevent the sale of all but a very limited range of necessary items to the public. Naturally the legislation preserved in amber the preferences of the late 1940s despite their inappropriateness in the 1960s, 1970s and 1980s. Tripe and ice cream could be purchased, but not

---

[1] See Ralph Harris and Arthur Seldon, *Shoppers' Choice*, IEA Occasional Paper 68, 1984; Terry Burke and J.R. Shackleton, *Sunday, Sunday: The Issues in Sunday Trading*, Adam Smith Institute, 1989, and 'The Sunday Trading Battle in England and Wales', *Journal of Interdisciplinary Economics*, Vol.4, 1992; John Burton, *Whither Sunday Trading? The Case for Deregulation*, Hobart Paper No.123, Institute of Economic Affairs, 1993.

frozen vegetables and fish fingers. Other anomalies reflected types of retail outlet: thus newspapers could be sold, but not bibles, fresh cream but not evaporated milk.

Such anomalies, together with the decline of religious observance and changing lifestyles, led to over 20 unsuccessful attempts to reform the law. In an object lesson for students of economic regulation, all these attempts failed because a coalition of special interests resisted the public's frequently-expressed desire for reform. The issue came to a head after 1986, when a government-supported Bill, following a wide-ranging Committee of Inquiry's recommendation, was defeated on its Second Reading (only the second defeat at this stage on a government bill since 1924). At a time when Mrs Thatcher's Government was at the height of its powers, 72 Conservative backbenchers defied a three-line whip. Her defeat was brought about by a bizarre alliance of trade unionists, traditionalists, Sabbatarians and selected business interests, plus no doubt a little mischief from the Opposition benches.

Following this defeat, the Sunday trading legislation rapidly fell into disrepute and, in many localities, into virtual disuse. Retailers – even, towards the end, many of the big multiples which had earlier been against Sunday trading – either opened with little fear of prosecution by tolerant local authorities or, with varying degrees of success, challenged the status of the English law through the courts.

By 1993-94 it was widely accepted that change was inevitable. However, in the event, a compromise was reached which fell some way short of complete deregulation. Parliament allowed unlimited Sunday opening for small stores but restricted larger ones to six hours opening – a compromise which actually had the effect of *reducing* the opening hours of large supermarkets in areas where *de facto* deregulation had previously existed. Since then, the Government has liberalised weekday opening hours and has introduced longer periods of sale of alcohol on Sunday. Nevertheless, the restrictions which remain preclude widespread round-the-clock supermarket operation of the kind which exists in some parts of the United States. Moreover, by favouring smaller firms they may prevent some of the advantages of large-scale operation being achieved. There is still a strong argument for complete deregulation of opening hours, but it is unlikely to be a priority with legislators for the foreseeable future.

Consumer Protection

For centuries[2] it has been argued that the consumer needs protection against unscrupulous retailers. Instead of the principle of *caveat emptor*, it has been claimed that the state needs to intervene in a variety of ways. A partial listing of the classes of legislation with which UK retailers have to deal includes: food quality and hygiene, false descriptions, consumer credit, labelling of dangerous products, statement of and control of prices, inaccurate quantities and hallmarking of precious metals.[3] The separate pieces of primary legislation, together with associated regulations, run into the hundreds. In the UK legislation is principally the responsibility of the Department of Trade and Industry (although increasingly the initiative derives from Brussels).[4] Local enforcement is in the hands of trading standards departments.

The economic rationale for consumer protection legislation lies in the problems associated with imperfect information in product markets. For many products, information is asymmetric; producers know more about the good than consumers. Although in some cases the consumer can acquire information cheaply by sampling the product, for many goods the cost deters experimentation. More seriously, for some goods, even after sampling the consumer may be little the wiser. For example, food which tastes acceptable may contain additives which damage health in the long term; dangerous toys may appear harmless; and nightclothes may give no

---

[2] Standardisation of weights and measures for products such as wine, ale and widths of cloth appears in Magna Carta.

[3] See B.W. Harvey and D.L. Parry, *The Law of Consumer Protection and Fair Trading*, 4th edition, London, Dublin and Edinburgh: Butterworth, 1992.

[4] The Directorate-General for Environment and Consumer Protection was set up in 1981, following on from earlier adoption of 'consumer entitlements' in relation to health and safety, information and education, and so forth. Under this rubric a steady flow of Directives has been issued on such topics as foodstuffs, product liability and misleading advertising. (See Duncan Law, *The Framework of Consumer Protection in the UK*, Polytechnic of Central London Research Working Paper 40, 1990. For a case study of the slaughterhouse industry see Richard North, *Death by Regulation: The Butchery of the British Meat Industry*, Health Series No.12, IEA Health and Welfare Unit, 1993.)

indication of being highly inflammable. State intervention on behalf of the consumer to mandate full information disclosure[5] and regulate product standards may seem desirable. A case can also be made for regulation on behalf of 'good' producers. The argument here is that, in the absence of any means of telling good products from bad, consumers may simply steer clear of that class of products altogether. In this sense, 'bad products drive out good', as Akerlof has put it,[6] with both producers and consumers the losers.

However, this conclusion does not necessarily follow.[7] Free markets are capable of generating consumer protection mechanisms of their own, including consumer interest groups such as the Consumer's Association which disseminates information about product standards. More importantly, retailers can offer a form of insurance to consumers about quality and value for money in the form of warranties, guarantees and pledges.[8] Such devices act as a powerful signal to consumers that the product is of an acceptable quality and that the retailer is 'here to stay'.[9] More generally, retailer reputation, product branding, 'kitemarking' to British

---

[5] The meaning of 'full' information is of course problematic. Information is rarely costless, and is something of which there can be too much as well as too little. It has recently been argued that we need more detail on food labelling; in addition to information about colourings and other additives, an environmental impact statement should be included. While the cost of this could be relatively small, the danger is that environmental claims made by manufacturers and retailers would have to be expensively demonstrated. Some Labour Party activists, for example, have argued for an inspectorate to check the validity of descriptions such as 'free range' for eggs and 'outdoor-reared' for meat. (See Nigel Griffiths, MP, 'Consumer Column', *Labour Party News*, June 1995.)

[6] G. Akerlof, 'The Market for Lemons: Qualitative Uncertainty and the Market Mechanism', *Quarterly Journal of Economics*, Vol.84, 1970, pp.488-500.

[7] See G. Heal, 'Do Bad Products Drive Out Good?', *Quarterly Journal of Economics*, Vol.90, 1976, pp.499-502. Heal points out that Akerlof's formal model of the problem resembles the classic 'prisoner's dilemma' of game theory. While this model indeed points to an undesirable outcome if the game is only played once, it does not follow that the same result would occur if the game is played repeatedly: the 'supergame' outcome is likely to be more positive.

[8] Such as the John Lewis Partnership's famous 'never knowingly undersold' promise, where it promises to refund price differences between its products and those sold in rival establishments.

[9] S. Grossman, 'The Informational Role of Warranties and Private Disclosure About Product Quality', *Journal of Law and Economics*, Vol.24, 1981, pp.461-83.

Standards and advertising constitute important indirect forms of consumer protection.

For example, customers can have a high degree of confidence in products sold by major retailers such as Marks & Spencer or Sainsbury's: legislation is largely unnecessary to enforce standards here. This is because incidents where goods were found to be dangerous or not of 'merchantable quality'[10] would certainly be widely publicised, with seriously adverse effects on these companies' reputation (their major competitive advantage) and therefore ultimately on their sales.

'Reputation' is a term which can be used widely to refer to attributes of goods which consumers value. For example, some consumers are particularly concerned, as we have seen, about environmental issues.[11] The Co-op has recently gained some competitive advantage by announcing a policy of honesty and openness in describing the 'green' status of its products. Smaller producers or retailers can achieve the same effect by submitting to assessment from private bodies such as the Soil Association, which will (for example) certificate Free Range eggs.[12]

A firm or product's reputation needs to be established over time. However, once achieved, it can often be profitably transferred into new fields. We have already spoken of Marks & Spencer's movement into financial services. Richard Branson's reputation under the Virgin name has also proved to be transferable – from record retailing to air travel to radio to soft drinks and even, like Marks & Spencer, into financial services.[13] Virgin also intends to relaunch the MGM cinema chain in a completely new format.

One way to achieve reputation fairly quickly is through advertising. As Nelson[14] has pointed out, heavy advertising

---

[10] This old-fashioned expression, first introduced in UK legislation in 1893, was defined in the 1973 Supply of Goods (Implied Terms) Act as 'fit for the purpose or purposes for which goods of that kind are commonly bought', bearing in mind 'any description applied to them, the price (if relevant) and all the relevant circumstances'. Legislation is shortly to be introduced using a more modern term, 'satisfactory quality' (see *The Guardian*, 4 February 1995).

[11] Further explored in the next section.

[12] See Jonathan Glancey, 'Are you shopping soundly?', *The Independent*, 29 April 1995.

[13] C. German, 'Branson's PEP brings in £42m', *The Independent*, 7 April 1995.

[14] P. Nelson, 'Advertising and Information', *Journal of Political Economy*, 1974, pp.729-54.

[64]

(however limited its apparent informational content) is often regarded by the public as a signal that a product is of a good quality. Consumers may reason that an expensive advertising campaign will pay dividends only if newly-attracted customers are satisfied and make repeat purchases. Firms can be optimistic about this only if they feel that the product is a good one. Thus 'the more a brand advertises, the more likely it is to be a better buy'.[15]

In order to justify continuing reputations, producers and retailers need to institute procedures to maintain quality – this has been the endlessly reiterated lesson of the total quality management movement in the last decade. In effect, as Kay and Vickers have argued,[16] large firms must develop internal regulation of product standards – which may be more effective than externally-imposed regulation,[17] especially as they are competing with other firms to maintain high levels of quality.

One implication is that a retailing sector increasingly characterised by competition between a number of large players stands less in need of regulation and the imposition of mandatory quality standards than a more atomistic sector. Large retailers, being more visible, have more of a reputation to lose than smaller players. Moreover, the alternative of imposing common government regulation across the sector may lead to disproportionately high compliance costs for smaller outlets (for example, having to instal a particular type of refrigerated display cabinet for the storage of small quantities of fresh food). By forcing smaller retailers out of business, it may thus reduce competition. It is also arguable that some element of consumer choice is lost when quality is mandated.[18]

---

[15] *Ibid.*, p.732.

[16] J. Kay and J. Vickers, 'Regulatory reform in Britain', *Economic Policy*, Vol.7, 1988, p.322.

[17] State certification of products almost always takes a monopoly form. Over time this may discourage innovation as entrepreneurs find new products or processes run up against bureaucratically-applied standards.

[18] Quality is a 'good', something which people value. However, like all goods, it has a price. People may prefer to settle for a lower quality at a lower price. They may choose to eat in cheap restaurants, to shop in open markets, to buy secondhand clothes rather than new ones – particularly if their incomes are low. In more cases than is sometimes thought, consumers are perfectly capable of assessing quality variations for themselves – and 'quality regulation in such a case limits consumer choice'. (Kay and Vickers, *op. cit.*, p.320.)

Against this background, it is tempting to reiterate Christina Fulop's conclusion all those years ago: 'it is doubtful whether the public interest would be furthered by a wholesale extension of present [consumer protection] regulations'.[19] In view of the large number of extra rules and directives on consumer protection which have appeared in recent years from the European Commission, it may even be that the marginal returns from government regulation are now negative.[20]

Retail Location

Another long-standing form of government intervention is influence over the location of various types of economic activity. Retailing has been no exception. These powers have not been used as frequently as in some other countries, but plenty of examples can be found.

The number of retail pharmacies in any area is rationed by entry controls operated by local Family Health Service Authorities in the award of NHS dispensing contracts. These controls, which were introduced in 1987, are meant to contain the rising cost of pharmaceutical services, while at the same time ensuring adequate access.[21] In Soho, the local authority restricts the number of sex shops. In Hampstead, Camden Council resisted for many years the introduction of fast-food retailer MacDonalds, which was felt likely to lower the tone of this exclusive neighbourhood. Often the pressure for such restrictions comes from other retailers as much as the general public.

A location issue now much debated is the drift towards out-of-town shopping in superstores and malls. As explained in Section II, the share of such locations in total retail spending

---

[19] C. Fulop, *Revolution in Retailing, op. cit.*, p.34.

[20] In 1993, 776,000 consumer complaints were made via local Trading Standards Departments: the number of such complaints is growing at nearly 10 per cent per annum. It is difficult to believe that the quality of goods and services is worsening as dramatically as this seems to imply.

[21] The National Audit Office report, *Community Pharmacies in England and Wales*, 1992 (pp.3-4), found that 'Entry controls have been successful in halting the growth in the number of pharmacies. But the controls leave existing pharmacies untouched, irrespective of their contribution to the accessibility of the service'.

rose sharply in the late 1980s; by contrast, traditional high street locations saw their market share decline. In the recent recession absolute falls have occurred in high street retail spending, and an exodus of well-known multiples seems to have been occurring – some as a result of deliberate relocation to out-of-town sites, others as a result of closure.

This trend continued into the first quarter of 1995, which saw the high street losing one substantial chain, with two more in difficulty. Rumbelows, the electrical retailers, ceased to trade, while Dewhurst (the 'master butcher' arm of the Vestey family's meat business) and Dillons book stores went into receivership.

- With Rumbelows, the problem appears to have been a straightforward one of comparative disadvantage in location, relative to edge-of-town electrical retailers, which are able to offer easy parking and immediate sales from stock.

- With Dewhurst, the problem seems to have been a persistent loss of trade over time to supermarkets and superstores, which seem able to match the traditional butcher in price, choice and quality. On grounds of convenience alone, modern households evidently wish to combine the purchases of meats, dairy products, vegetables and packaged foods in a single weekly visit.

- With Dillons, however, the problem is said to have been rents which were too high, as the group bid its way into prime shopping locations. Books are simply not capable of generating the margins and turnover available from, say, clothing sales.

High streets in many parts of the country are therefore changing their appearance. In lucky cases, new types of retailing – for example, catering for tourists – or service uses have taken over the sites vacated by older retailers. In less favoured areas, boarded-up shops, video rental shops or short-term lets to charity shops or auction stores predominate.

Critical comment has been widespread. The House of Commons Select Committee on the Environment, for example, has been a channel for much complaint. The Committee, according to its chairman, Barry Field, MP, has taken the view that retail development policies have allowed

[67]

'the building of too many superstores and other large retail developments in locations which are inappropriate on environmental, heritage and social grounds'.[22]

Building on greenfield sites has, it is claimed, destroyed the character of large areas of the countryside, and generated substantial volumes of car traffic which might not otherwise have existed. By sucking economic activity out of the high street, it is said to have destroyed the character of many old market towns in particular.

In its well-publicised October 1994 report,[23] the Select Committee argued that developers should have to demonstrate that their proposals would not harm town centres. The onus should be on them to prove (how?) that no harm would be caused to existing interest groups. In the committee's view, all applications for developments around market towns should have to be accompanied by a full assessment of their likely impact on the catchment area. Further, planning permission should not be given if a suitable site existed within or close to the town centre. The policy should cover all forms of out-of-town retailing, including warehouse clubs, which to the Committee resemble low-price, limited-range department stores. There also appears in the Committee's report to be a general presumption against factory outlet centres.[24]

The report recognised that positive steps might also have to be taken to encourage people to travel by public transport to the town centre, rather than by private car to the out-of-town shopping centre. The problem, as the Committee saw it, is not just that, say, large grocery stores draw custom from other grocery retailers. It was noted that large food retailers have broadened their range to include in-house bakeries, butchery counters, fishmongers and so on (with consequences for traditional retailers which are apparent from Table 10). They have indeed gone beyond this to move into many non-food items. The Committee was particularly concerned that the current wide distribution of chemists and post offices, held to

---

[22] Press Notice issued by the Committee Office of the House of Commons, 1 November 1994, giving statement by the Committee Chairman, Mr Barry Field, MP for the Isle of Wight.

[23] House of Commons Environment Committee, *Shopping Centres and their Future*, London: HMSO, October 1994.

[24] House of Commons Environment Committee, *ibid.*, paras.76,77,82 and 86.

TABLE 10:
Market Share of Specialist Retailers, 1984 and 1994
(Percentages of Relevant Markets)

	1984	1994
Butchers	41·5	22·0
Fishmongers	54·0	33·6
High Street Bakers	28·0	8·0
Milk Deliveries	83·0	50·0

Source: The Observer, 26 March 1995.

possess a social utility beyond private profitability, might be threatened by the ever-broadening scope of the superstores.

Early in 1995 these conclusions were given some support from government-funded research[25] by the Urban and Economic Development Group. Its study, for the Department of the Environment, suggested that only 3 per cent of market towns are thriving, the vast majority being in danger of falling into a 'spiral of decline'. The research, which covered 338 towns and cities in England and Wales, suggested that one in seven towns is actually declining. The culprit was identified as the out-of-town store, aided and abetted by transport policies favouring the private car.

It is clear that out-of-town superstores would be impossible in their current form without widespread car use. Critics of the superstores claim that increased car use associated with the shift to out-of-town shopping has led to increased air pollution and congestion. One calculation shows that a typical out-of-town superstore imposes external costs in excess of £25,000 per week.[26]

Government policy on out-of-town development has wavered. The Environment Secretary, John Gummer, appeared initially to accept the Select Committee diagnosis. *The Times* of 5 November 1994, reporting an unsuccessful appeal by Safeway against refusal of planning permission to build an out-of-town superstore near Andover, noted that the rejection was based on

---

[25] 'Britain's market towns in decline as superstores rise', *The Independent*, 12 February 1995.

[26] Hugh Raven and Tim Lang with Caroline Dumonteil, *Off Our Trolleys? Food Retailing and the Hypermarket Economy, op. cit.*, p.11.

'...the potential inconvenience to people without cars and ... the site did not meet the [Environment] Department's guidelines requiring that stores improve the "vitality and viability" of town centres'.[27]

However, in a speech to the Retail Consortium (24 January 1995) the Prime Minister, John Major, took a rather different line. He was quoted as saying:

'New development is necessary. I know it is often controversial, but we can't treat our towns and villages as museums of the past. Our policy is not to smother investment in either town or country. We have introduced tougher tests for out-of-town development, but we haven't padlocked the gate to every new greenfield site. Survival was never achieved by standing still. Town centres themselves must adapt whatever their size.'

An attempt was made to smooth over the apparent differences between the Prime Minister and the Secretary of State. A Department of the Environment spokesperson said:

'The policy is to encourage the allocation of shops next to existing shopping centres, but there may be circumstances where an out-of-town centre is more suitable. There is no moratorium on them.'[28]

However, Mr Gummer subsequently restated his harder line. On 19 July 1995 he issued draft planning guidelines which made it clear that further planning permissions for out-of-town developments were unlikely. Speaking on BBC Radio, he said:

'I want people to be able to live and shop and work and worship and take leisure at the centre of town. If it can't be done there, perhaps there is somewhere reasonably near that can be used and only after that can one see an "out of town" result.'[29]

---

[27] At around the same time, the press also reported a predictable rush to build hundreds of retail parks, shopping centres and superstores before their previously-granted planning permissions (which are valid for only three years) ran out. Many of these projects had previously been of doubtful viability, but with a freeze on future out-of-town developments apparently imminent, they unexpectedly acquired a scarcity value. (See Catherine Pepinster, 'Rush to build out-of-town malls', The Independent on Sunday, 18 December 1994.)

[28] Stephen Bates, 'Major pledges to ease drink sales law – Out-of-town shops back in the running', The Guardian, 25 January 1995.

[29] James Meikle, 'Gummer's salvo for town centres', The Guardian, 20 July 1995.

The Case Against Re-regulation of Location

There appears, therefore, to be a strong political feeling against out-of-town retailing, and a belief that shopping location (after a brief period of deregulation) should be re-regulated. Some of this concern may be because people are unclear on the basic facts. Tesco has pointed out that of 102 stores which it has opened since 1990, less than half were on green field sites; 20 per cent were constructed on contaminated land unlikely to be used for anything else.[30] Nevertheless, the concern appears so widespread that the case against Mr Gummer's position needs a brief restatement.

- Interfering with consumers' revealed preferences in order to offset perceived social problems – such as unequal access by non-car-owners to out-of-town sites – is economically inefficient. If these problems *are* serious (and there is as yet no convincing evidence that they are), subsidised public transport for old-age pensioners, for example, is likely to be a more efficient solution than forcing people to shop in town centres.

- Regulation to prevent out-of-town expansion creates arbitrary gains and losses. Gainers will include existing out-of-town retailers who will be exempt from new competition, as well as the high-street retailers regulation is meant to protect. Other beneficiaries will include those who own retail sites (those owning out-of-town sites with existing planning permission as well as landlords of urban sites). Retailers in rented property will pay higher rents in the long run. Consumers in some parts of the country where out-of-town retailing has been slower to develop will suffer from restricted choice, while those where it is already well-established will not be affected – although it is this group which has caused the alleged problem!

- The wider environmental consequences are unclear. If people who wish to shop outside town are forced instead to shop in the high street, the increased congestion and pollution from traffic in towns may be at least as problematic as that created by out-of-town retailing –

---

[30] London Economics, *The Grocery Retailing Revolution, op. cit.*, p.35.

especially as the smaller scale of high-street shops is likely to mean less efficient transport of stocks. In any case, using regulation and prohibition to deal with problems of pollution and congestion is likely to be a second-best solution compared with road pricing or other market-based solutions. Only around 12 per cent of car mileage is devoted to shopping, and much of this would not be affected if shoppers had to drive into town for their purchases instead. As driving in towns is typically slower than driving outside towns, pollution is unlikely to fall in line with the reduced distance travelled.

- Giving planners greater powers to regulate land use to protect the 'vitality and viability of the town centre' raises a host of problems, from NIMBYism (Not In My Back Yard) to special interest pleading, to potential corruption.

But Are Retail Rents the Problem?

In any case, the belief that the malaise in Britain's high streets is directly related to the growth of out-of-town shopping may be an over-simplification. As suggested in the previous section, it has been plausibly argued that many of the problems of retailing in this country come from excessively high rents. This argument deserves spelling out at some length, for to many economists such a view may appear counter-intuitive: in a simple version of Ricardo's theory of rent,[31] the landlord appropriates all, or almost all, the retail profits in excess of those required just to stay in business (the economist's notion of 'normal profit'). Surely a fall in retailing profitability means a fall in rents, and therefore rents cannot be a determining factor in the health of the high street?

John Burton, however, has claimed that retail rents tend to rise almost regardless of trading conditions as a result of the peculiar English and Welsh legal and institutional system of setting commercial rents. Professor Burton concludes that

---

[31] In *An Essay on the Influence of a Low Price of Corn and the Profit of Stock* (1815: see Volume IV of *The Works and Correspondence of David Ricardo*, ed. P. Sraffa, Cambridge University Press, 1951), David Ricardo argued that higher revenues from enhanced productivity in agriculture would go to landlords in the form of higher rents in the long run: only 'normal' profits would remain with the cultivator. In an analogous manner, landlords of retail properties could be expected to be the ultimate beneficiaries of productivity gains in retailing.

'the juggernaut of rent increases ... has major effects on the character of many shopping areas in terms of tenant mix and the vibrancy and variety that they afford both the shopper and the pavement stroller or window shopper'.[32]

As a House of Commons motion,[33] moved by Sir David Steel, noted, these effects threaten the historic identity of local communities, including areas of national interest.

The English and Welsh[34] commercial retail lease has a number of curious features:

- it is long term – typically 25 years – during which time the tenant is responsible for the repair, maintenance and insurance of the premises;

- it includes a rent review clause – typically at five-year intervals – which stipulates that rent reviews are upwards only and are not subject to any external third party approval.

The long-term lease meets the needs of institutions (principally the big life and pension funds) for low-risk long-term investment, providing a 'clean' income flow, net of any outgoings. In other European countries leases are shorter, with the landlord shouldering some or all of the responsibility for the upkeep and upgrading of the building.[35] (See Box 3)

The upwards-only rent review is supposed to be based on what the premises would be worth on an open market. The justification for the upwards-only clause is that continuous inflation is assumed, thus overriding any changes in market prices resulting from a falling demand for town centre retail

---

[32] John Burton, *Retail Rents*, London: Adam Smith Institute, 1992, p.3.

[33] 15 October 1990. A motion moved by Sir David Steel, and three other backbench MPs from across the three main parties, expressed concern about 'increases in commercial rents significantly above inflation' making it 'extremely difficult for independent and specialist traders to survive'.

[34] Different systems operate in Scotland and Northern Ireland.

[35] Another disadvantage which retailers faced in the English and Welsh legal system has just been removed (after 328 years), although its influence will linger on existing leases. 'Privity of contract', which made the first owner of a commercial lease liable for rents unpaid by successor tenants, has been abolished by a private member's bill for which the British Retail Consortium has lobbied for many years.

[73]

BOX 3

How Things are Done in France and Germany

Restrictions on retail location, like other forms of market regulation, seem more highly developed on the Continent than in the UK.

In France a moratorium on the further development of out-of-town shopping was introduced in 1993. It is said to be a reaction to pressure from small shopkeepers and others concerned about the impact on traditional retail patterns.

To date environmental concerns have played little part in French planning decisions. Under the 1973 Loi Royer, commercial developments are approved by the Ministry of Industry and Economic Development on commercial grounds and by the local Mayor on planning grounds. In 1992 under the Loi Sapin, the consideration of commercial issues was transferred from the Ministry to a committee of local commune mayors, and representatives of chambers of commerce and consumer groups.

Out-of-town developments were said to have had a severe impact on town centres, particularly on the smaller towns. Officials were inclined to place responsibility for these on the (rival) mayors who took the planning decisions.

In contrast, in the German town of Freiburg, the Committee found a strong town plan, which focused some forms of retailing (food, flowers, clothes, shoes, textiles) in town centres, while permitting out-of-town development for bulkier items (DIY, furniture, carpets, car parts). This highly directed, even authoritarian, approach had been adopted, in a less restrictive form, by about 30 German towns.

Source: House of Commons Select Committee, *Shopping Centres and Their Future*, Annex IV, pp.lx-lxx, London: HMSO, October 1994.

space. The tenant benefits not only from the security of a long lease, but from a lower rent as only a minimal allowance has to be made for landlord's risk. The alternative to the long lease with reviews is a series of shorter leases; these are common in other countries, although any increases are normally subject to some form of official arbitration, which takes account of an index of costs and any improvements the landlord has made to the property.

In England and Wales the rent is set at the level a hypothetical landlord and tenant would agree, without reference to actual trading conditions. This fictional market rent is determined by an appeal to 'comparable' properties – that is, to recently agreed rents for similar properties.

There are thus two quite separate sectors for commercial rents in England and Wales – a small open market sector for new lettings (estimated by Burton at 4 per cent of total lettings) and a large rent-administered sector, with rents set by administrative procedures, which are meant to mimic the workings of a hypothetical market. They fail to do so, however, with the result that the upwards-only rent review process builds an element of core inflation into retail prices. Town-centre retailers in particular face rising costs over time.

The upshot of Burton's argument is that the proximate cause of the problems of the high street may have been wrongly diagnosed: it is possible that the retail rent situation is a more important factor than the exodus of major food retailers to out-of-town sites in bringing about current difficulties.

Be that as it may, it seems unlikely that the long-term change in shopping patterns can be reversed by government fiat. As we have seen, car ownership, home ownership, freezers, microwaves and the changing lifestyles associated with them have revolutionised shopping patterns. For very many people, the weekly or fortnightly trip to the superstore to stock up on food makes obvious sense. So does the trip to an out-of-town location to buy furniture packs, hi-fis and do-it-yourself equipment. Cars cannot easily be taken into Britain's old town centres (indeed, their use in towns should perhaps be discouraged) and without cars, taking home bulky purchases is well-nigh impossible. As a Tesco spokesperson said, in response to Mr Gummer's new planning guidelines:

> 'Millions of people shop in superstores each week because it suits the way they live. The guidance fits oddly with the Government's attitude to deregulation in other policy areas.'[36]

Traditional town centres and high streets are not necessarily doomed. Successful high streets will attract businesses – such as financial services, travel agents, clothing specialists, hairdressers, restaurants, delicatessens and entertainment facilities – which can conveniently serve their public in a

---

[36] James Meikle, 'Gummer's salvo for town centres', *op. cit.*

central location where cars are less necessary and there is no
need to carry home bulky purchases.

V. OTHER ENVIRONMENTAL ISSUES

Further concerns about the wider environmental impact of retailing trends have recently attracted attention and have perhaps been most powerfully articulated in the Institute for Public Policy Research's publication *Off our Trolleys?*.[1] The chief complaint is against food retailers, but many of the strictures apply to a greater or lesser degree to hypermarkets and superstores of all kinds. Some of the IPPR's concerns were discussed in Section III above. Here we focus on three other themes – the generation of waste, the industrialisation of horticulture, and the increase in food imports from less-developed countries.

Generation of Waste

Extensive throwaway packaging is a feature of modern retailing, as Christina Fulop was already beginning to observe in the early 1960s. This packaging is costly to produce; it is said to add 'about ten per cent extra' to prices,[2] and uses energy and non-renewable natural resources. The *disposal* of waste packaging by households is also costly, both in terms of the capital and labour used in its collection and in the environmental degradation associated with storing, recycling, burying or incinerating it. These disposal costs are not borne by the retailer, but by the general public in terms of taxation and environmental damage; consequently, it is contended, packaging is carried beyond the socially optimal level.

The existence of such 'external costs' is said to give rise to a market failure which justifies government intervention. The authors of *Off our Trolleys?*, together with organisations like Friends of the Earth,[3] claim that government intervention has been inadequate, partly because of lobbying by retailing interests. Whether or not such lobbying has been significant is

---

[1] By Hugh Raven and Tim Lang with Caroline Dumonteil, *op. cit.*

[2] Consumers' Association estimate, cited in Raven *et al.*, p.16.

[3] *The Guardian*, 15 July 1995.

TABLE 11:
People Who Were 'Very Worried' About
Various Environmental Issues, 1993

Issue	% of Respondents
Chemicals in rivers/seas	63
Toxic waste	63
Radioactive waste	60
Losing 'green belt' land	35
Traffic congestion	35
Fouling by dogs	29
Household waste disposal	22
Not enough recycling	19

Source: Social Trends, 1995.

debatable: public concern over the issue appears from Table 11 to rate well below worries about dogs fouling footpaths and parks. The public's ranking of concerns may be perfectly rational. Although UK households generate 20 million tonnes of waste per year, only a proportion of this arises from 'excess' packaging – and household waste in any case accounts for less than 15 per cent of total solid waste.

The IPPR report argues that we need 'mandatory packaging reduction targets' and the encouragement of re-usable and refillable containers (which are said to be underused in the UK compared with most of our European neighbours) rather than recycling, landfill and the use of incinerated waste for energy generation. It claims also that the Trades Descriptions Act needs modification to cover what it sees as misleading claims that packaging is 'environment-friendly'.

Packaging – Costs and Benefits

A number of observations need to be made here. *First*, the fact that packaging is costly is not a problem in itself. Economists argue that if a good is purchased, its value to the consumer is normally at least as great as its cost, whether measured in monetary or resource terms. Forty years ago, many grocery products were weighed and wrapped by hand. This was time-consuming and often unhygienic. It led to very considerable product waste in itself: sugar was spilt, biscuits were broken,

[78]

exposed food deteriorated quickly. Manufacturers and retailers investing in pre-packing food and other products gained market share as consumers came to prefer to buy their groceries in this way – even if it cost slightly more. Moreover, attractive packaging is an essential aspect of advertising and marketing products; consequent increases in sales make possible economies of scale which can be expected to lead, in competitive markets, to lower prices.

So it is not obvious that a world with no pre-packaged food would ultimately be one of lower grocery prices. Furthermore, the consumer is not obliged to buy heavily packaged food. It is still possible to buy many products – fish, meat, vegetables, fruit, bread, cakes – in the 'traditional' manner. Moreover, most big food retailers offer a range of basic groceries in 'no frills' packaging, at substantially reduced prices. The popularity of heavily packaged foods and other products suggests that consumers obtain some benefit from packaging, rather than that it is foisted upon them by malign producer interests.

The point that is made about external costs is more telling. Notwithstanding the benefits which may accrue to consumers from pre-packed products, packaging may be carried too far if the prices which consumers pay do not cover the disposal as well as the production costs of goods.

Problems of this kind have been explored by economists for many years.[4] The solutions they have favoured typically involve measures to 'internalise' external costs – to ensure that the private costs of economic activity are brought in line with the broader social costs. This can be done in a number of ways, for example by reassigning property rights[5] or by imposing taxes on the activity which creates external costs. A tax on excess packaging might be appropriate in principle, though probably extremely difficult to design. A more promising type of

---

[4] A classic early exploration of the problem of externalities – the divergence of private from social costs and benefits – is found in A. C. Pigou, *The Economics of Welfare*, London: Macmillan, 1920.

[5] For example, dumping of rubbish on common land will be greatly reduced if rights to the land are assigned to an individual or organisation who can then use the law against those doing the dumping. The elaboration of this principle is owed to Ronald H. Coase, 'The problem of social cost', *Journal of Law and Economics*, Vol.3, October 1960, pp.1-44.

taxation is the government's proposed tax on landfill, foreshadowed in the recent Environment Bill.[6]

The proposals put forward by Raven, Lang and Dumonteil, however, seem difficult to justify. 'Mandatory packaging reduction targets'[7] are vague and likely to be arbitrary. As firms use different types of packing and employ combinations of different materials, the disposal costs bear no simple relation to weight or other common attributes. Insisting on a common standard would have very different implications for different producers: some would have readily available alternative ways of packing and presenting products, while others would not. Firms (and consumers) would be penalised in an unsystematic way: it is not obvious that the outcome would be an improvement.

Similarly, re-use and refill systems for drinks are one way of reducing some of the costs associated with packaging, but no evidence is adduced to show that widespread use of returnable glass bottles would be preferable to disposable plastic ones when all the relevant costs (collecting, washing, and so on) are taken into account. Sainsbury's view is that the increased weight associated with returnable glass bottles would mean a reduction in the average size of bottles, and thus an increase in the total amount of packaging. This is dismissed by the IPPR authors as special pleading – yet a report from British Glass (surely another interested party?) arguing that returnable bottles are more energy-efficient is cited with approval.[8] This determination to see large retailers and packaging producers as villains is also apparent in these authors' attitude towards the subsidised recycling schemes and recycling collection points[9] which the private sector has provided in recent years: these are seen as a very poor substitute

---

[6] Ideally this would raise costs to local authorities which would then pass them on in collection charges to households and businesses. This in turn would encourage the use of equipment such as domestic rubbish impactors and/or encourage households to switch their purchases to less packaging-intensive products.

[7] Probably a contradiction in terms: can a target be mandatory?

[8] Raven et al., op. cit., p.18.

[9] Tesco, for example, has recently announced a plan to open nine recycling centres. ('Tesco recycling centres will create 700 jobs', The Times, 27 September 1995.)

TABLE 12:
Percentage of Materials Recycled, 1990-94,
and Targets for 2000

	1990	1992	1994	2000 (targets)
Paper and Board	31	34	na	
Waste Paper Used in Newsprint	27	31	na	40
Glass	21	26	30	50
Aluminium Cans	6	16	24	50
Steel Cans	9	12	na	
Plastics	2	5	na	

Sources: Social Trends, Department of the Environment.

for the solutions they prefer.

There has been a significant increase in recycling in the UK in recent years (see Table 12). Recycling is, of course, likely to be more popular when market incentives work in the same direction as government policy. As the price of newsprint and of woodpulp rises, for example, collecting old newspapers for recycling becomes economically rational. In some areas this has apparently led to newspapers being stolen from recycling points.[10]

The Government has accepted European Packaging Directive targets for 'recovery' (recycling and producing energy through combustion of waste) of some materials, and in the Environment Bill it has taken powers to impose specific orders on producers to design products for reuse and recycling.

It is not our concern in this *Hobart Paper* to develop a detailed examination of alternative policies to deal with the problem of household waste disposal. We are simply concerned to point out that the issue is much more complex than critics of the superstores suggest. Policy needs to be designed with an understanding of why waste is generated and of the pattern of economic incentives associated with waste disposal, rather than with a preconceived view that waste is an evil to be suppressed at all costs.

---

[10] 'Thieves make a profit as public spirit turns to paper money', *The Guardian*, 15 July 1995.

The Industrialisation of Horticulture

Another environmental issue raised by the IPPR authors and others concerns the big retailers' move into selling fresh fruit and vegetables on a large scale, a move which in the 1980s led to an unprecedented range of fresh produce from all parts of the world becoming available in the larger stores and a considerable reduction in the share of traditional green-grocers and open markets.[11]

This has had, in the view of critics, a number of consequences. Large supermarkets have considerable buying power which they can exploit to force down the prices of fruit and vegetables. Concentration of nationwide distribution by the big retailers in a small number of depots has put a premium on suppliers who can supply large amounts of food to a consistent standard. Growers have had to invest in large-scale storage and packing facilities to meet the multiples' specifications. Thus, it is claimed smaller producers have been squeezed out and barriers to entry have been raised in horticulture. Another apparent consequence has been greater use of intensive methods of farming which employ large amounts of energy, together with additives and pesticides which may have long-term adverse consequences on health.

Demand for a uniform product has allegedly led to concentration on a limited range of varieties of fruits and vegetables. This in some areas has led to a virtual monoculture, which may have long-term adverse implications as genetic variation is reduced, crop disease and parasites flourish and there is an increased need for pesticides which may have damaging effects on the environment.[12]

Another result of the increasing power of the multiples is the growth of world-wide sourcing. Transport costs have fallen, and it is now profitable to import large amounts of produce

---

[11] In 1983 the multiples accounted for 24 per cent of the market. Today their share stands at over 50 per cent and is expected to rise to over 70 per cent by the end of the decade. Independent greengrocers have seen their share shrink from a third to less than a quarter. (Raven *et al.*, *op. cit.*, p.20.)

[12] This is indeed a worrying prospect, but it seems unlikely that the most appropriate way of avoiding it is to restrict food retailers' abilities to purchase from the sources they prefer. The economic pressures leading to intensive farming have been present for many years. They were associated, for example, with the development of the Common Agricultural Policy.

formerly home-grown. Domestic producers are, it is said, having to destroy perfectly good produce while seeing their local hypermarket sell similar fruit and vegetables flown in from thousands of miles away. Nor is this necessarily to the long-term benefit of food exporters, particularly those in poor countries, who allegedly see the structure of their economies distorted by the demands of Western retailers. As food journalist Colin Spencer wrote in a letter criticising newsreader Jeremy Paxman:

> 'If Mr Paxman stopped eating meat and dairy products and avoided all vegetables in supermarkets grown as cash crops from the Third World, and if he encouraged half the British population to follow him, he would find that Third World countries had enough protein grains...and enough land to grow their own indigenous crops to halt malnutrition and famine...As lack of food is a constant major factor in internecine wars and despotic régimes, such action...would undoubtedly save many human beings from suffering, death and imprisonment.'[13]

These criticisms seem to constitute a formidable indictment against the practices of the large food retailers. Yet are the criticisms wholly justified?

It must be true that the increased purchasing power of the large retailers will alter the structure of the market for fresh produce. Yet it remains to be demonstrated that it does so in a way which is counter to the 'public interest'. By encouraging the more efficient producers at the expense of the less efficient, retailers are acting as a positive force in the economy. By insisting on high and consistent product standards and investment in modern technologies for grading, storing and packing produce, retailers are contributing to the dynamism of the horticultural sector and the quality of its output. In principle, it is possible that such trends could go too far if one or two retailers came to possess monopsony[14] power. However, there is still very considerable competition among the major food retailers – suppliers are not completely at the mercy of the firms they supply. Indeed, if one of the claimed impacts of the fruit and vegetable retailing revolution

---

[13] Letter to *The Guardian*, 25 February 1995.

[14] A monopsony is a single buyer of a product, in contrast to a monopoly (a single seller).

is to increase the average scale of production it may produce its own countervailing power in the form of larger producers able to bargain with the majors on equal terms.

The argument that small suppliers are squeezed out is similar to the argument that small shops are squeezed out of retailing; it assumes that the existence of large numbers of small suppliers is an indicator of competition and therefore a good thing in itself, rather than a means to the end of promoting economic efficiency and consumer satisfaction. It also suffers from the same assumption that small producers are passive victims of change, rather than entrepreneurial individuals with the ingenuity to devise new methods of making a living and serving the public. Thus, although small food retailers greatly declined in numbers in the 1980s, the total number of small retailers actually rose as people moved into new business areas. Similarly, small suppliers of fruit and vegetables may be able to find new ways to make a living and new markets to explore.

In Japan, for example, 11 million people have joined the *Seikatsu* movement. In groups of no more than 200 they adopt a farm and buy its fresh seasonal produce, rather than rely on superstores. A similar project, known as Community Assisted Agriculture, where the farmer is hired to grow produce to a township's requirements, is taking hold in the USA despite the dominance of large-scale retailing. In this country, many small farmers are setting up stalls in town centres to sell their produce direct to the public. Some are developing a market niche in organic foodstuffs; there is a growing demand for 'alternative' food and vegetables produced by traditional methods. A recent development is the 'Box Scheme' where growers, in exchange for a guaranteed weekly order worth at least £5·00, deliver fresh vegetables direct to the shopper's door. Box Schemes selling organic produce are said to be flourishing in Exeter and Birmingham. Yet despite these developments in what she calls 'samizdat shopping', *The Guardian* commentator Joanna Coles accepts the IPPR argument and concludes 'it is high time the Monopolies and Mergers Commission stepped in'.[15] Quite what the MMC should do in order to reinstate older methods of sourcing retailing is not, however, made clear.

---

[15] Joanna Coles, 'Samizdat shopping beats the power of the supermarkets', *The Guardian*, 17 February 1995.

Trade Between Rich and Poor Countries

A final brief comment is necessary on the view that trade between rich and poor economies distorts the pattern of production in the latter. This seems to misunderstand the nature of uncoerced trade as a mutually beneficial activity from which both parties can gain. If food producers in less-developed countries find it profitable to export rather than produce for home consumption, the result is that more incomes – wages and profits – are generated and more can be imported (including other types of food).

What is the alternative? In the short run, abandoning trade with the developed economies would involve massive dislocation as workers lost their livelihoods and capital equipment specific to the production of the export crops became redundant. In the longer term, autarchy cuts producers off from competition, and thus tends to slow the growth of productivity which is the best hope for future prosperity.

The government planning of agriculture implied by the IPPR authors' policy prescription has not, to put it mildly, had a great deal of success in the post-war years. Price controls (to produce 'affordable' food for the cities), direction of investment and similar forms of regulation would surely, if the experience of 40 years of development economics teaches anything, result in very slow economic growth. Such slow economic growth in poor countries is more likely to produce the political and military conflict which people such as Colin Spencer fear.

Far from seeking to curb trade in foodstuffs between the UK and the Third World, there is a stronger case for increasing it – for instance by dismantling the European Union's Common Agricultural Policy, which greatly restricts our imports of food from poorer countries.

VI. CONCLUSIONS

The Contribution of Retailing

There is a long history of suspicion of retailing which stems partly from the view that retailers, unlike manufacturers and primary producers, add nothing of significance to the economy. This was formalised in Marx's distinction (which has, however, much earlier roots) between productive and unproductive labour. Employment in retailing, being part of the 'sphere of circulation of commodities', adds no value to production: it simply redistributes the 'surplus' generated by productive labour from one group of capitalists to another. Reasoning of this kind led the Soviet Union and its dependencies in Eastern Europe to downplay retailing and distribution in favour of heavy industry.[1] These economies typically had much smaller proportions of their labour forces engaged in retailing than Western economies.

Many of the problems of Soviet-style economies were linked to this attitude towards retailing. The drab shopping environments, limited opening hours, queues and poor service were not just minor details; they were manifestations of the fundamental unresponsiveness of these economies to consumer preferences and evidence of the planners' inability to match demand and supply. The experience of the command economies should remind us of the importance of a vibrant retail sector. Goods do not walk out of factories themselves, and production technology alone is insufficient to produce a rising living standard. Without an efficient and innovative retail sector, without firms competing to attract customers and offer them the most attractive products on offer, presented in a way which shows them to best advantage, the notion of consumer sovereignty remains an abstract and empty concept.

---

[1] Even today, Russia has only 200 supermarkets with a turnover of more than $2 million. Retail space per head of population is about a third of Western European levels. See 'A Survey of Russia's emerging market', *The Economist*, 8 April 1995.

It is not just anti-capitalist rhetoric that sees retailing as inferior to other forms of economic activity. In the recent deindustrialisation debate[2] it has often been asserted that employment in retailing and other service activities is not an adequate substitute for employment in manufacturing. Retailing has a reputation for offering less rewarding, less skilled and poorly paid work. The evidence suggests this is mistaken. The larger retailers offer career structures, training[3] and rates of pay[4] which compare favourably with many other industries. The sector as a whole offers major employment opportunities to groups which might otherwise find it difficult to obtain entry to the labour market: women, part-time workers, the self-employed (especially ethnic minorities), the young[5] and older workers.[6]

Another argument is that retailing contributes little to the UK's supposedly vital struggle in world markets. One riposte is that leading retailers such as Harrod's and Marks & Spencer make a significant contribution to the balance of payments by their sales to tourists and other visitors, and that British retailers (including Virgin, Body Shop and Sainsbury's) are now using their expertise to run major operations abroad which bring dividends to their British shareholders. Another response is the argument, well made by Professor Paul Krugman,[7] that what really determines a country's living standard is its level of productivity across the economy as a whole, not just in particular sectors. High productivity in retailing means that labour and other resources are available for employment in other sectors; conversely, a lower level of

---

[2] See N. Crafts, *Can Deindustrialisation Seriously Damage your Wealth?*, IEA Hobart Paper No.120, London: Institute of Economic Affairs, 1993.

[3] The retailing industry is amongst the largest users of the new National Vocational Qualifications.

[4] See London Economics, *The Grocery Retailing Revolution, op. cit.*, p.32.

[5] Part-time jobs in retailing are young people's most common form of first work experience.

[6] Do-it-yourself retailer B&Q has a policy favouring the recruitment of older workers, who are felt to be more sympathetic and helpful to the company's customers.

[7] P. Krugman, 'Competitiveness: a Dangerous Obsession', *Foreign Affairs*, Vol.73 (2), March-April 1994, pp.28-94.

retail productivity would divert resources from other sectors, including those which export a larger proportion of their value added.

Public Policy Conclusions

The evidence presented in this *Hobart Paper* points to UK retailing, despite a relatively high degree of concentration, being both dynamic and competitive. It is dynamic in the sense that new forms of retailing are constantly emerging, as old forms shrink or wither away; it is competitive in that barriers to entry are low, consumers are offered a choice of retailing bundles (price, range, quality, access, convenience, ambience), and the less successful retailers are subject to exit, regardless of the scale of their operation.

There are only two ways for retailers in such a competitive environment to capture higher-than-normal profits. They can either provide a premium service, for which customers are happy to pay a premium price; or they can hold their costs (labour, sites, operations, inventory) below those of their rivals. In a competitive market such as that of the UK, any advantage is likely to be short-lived, unless the retailer has a capacity to innovate ahead of the imitators, has robust relationships with all stakeholders and enjoys a durable reputation for quality, value and reliability. We have therefore argued, drawing on recent theoretical developments as well as empirical evidence, that concerns about the overall market structure in UK retailing are exaggerated: although there is a fairly small number of big players with large market shares, there is a high degree of competition from both traditional and new forms of retailing.

Recent concern has focussed on local rather than national markets, with the claim that the former are more highly concentrated and it is here that monopoly power is exercised. We reject this view. But, even were it accepted, it is difficult to see what policy conclusion would follow. The regulator's task would presumably be to break the local monopoly. How could this be done? One way might simply be to order the shop to cease trading, in the hope that two or more retailers would move into the vacated space. Another would be to order large retailers to lay on a free bus service into a neighbouring town, although it would be hard to compensate shoppers for their lost time – except possibly through money-off vouchers to be spent with the competition!

Another approach might be to order the monopoly store to franchise out various sections, so that it would lose any advantages of scale and scope in operation and marketing. Or it could be ordered to raise prices across the board. No doubt other regulatory proposals could be put forward.

These bizarre options have only to be listed to see how deeply unpopular they would be with local shoppers. There are no grounds for supposing such actions would return the market to its pre-monopoly position – even if that was felt to be desirable. It is more likely that the regulatory intervention would be used by (failing) competitors to boost their own trading positions at the expense of their rivals – a sure recipe for long-term stagnation.

Moving on from structural considerations, we surveyed the conduct of large retailers. The main issues involve supplier discounts to large retailers and exclusive dealing. In our view the response of the MMC and OFT on the former issue seems well-judged. But we are not entirely convinced of the extreme position that no regulatory watchdogs are required; it seems to us that some recent cases suggest that RPM-like refusals to supply remain a problem.

Turning to wider areas of concern, we have seen that a case continues to be made in Parliament and elsewhere for regulation of retail location and opening hours, and for further measures of consumer protection. We do not agree that further regulation is required; indeed, we would argue for significant deregulation in some areas. In particular, we are opposed to using regulatory powers to prevent the drift of certain types of retailing to out-of-town sites. If people clearly want to shop for bulky and heavy items in more convenient locations than the traditional high street, they should be enabled to do so wherever possible. Certainly, environmental considerations ought to be factored into firms' and households' decisions by making them responsible for measurable external costs which they impose on the community; we believe strongly, for example, in a road-pricing policy. However, such considerations apply across the board, and not just to large retailers.

The central policy question of the moment concerns the use of the planning process to limit out-of-town or edge-of-town development to situations where the would-be retailer is able to prove that the new superstore will have no impact on local shopping centres. Such a rule favours the existing edge-of-town retailers (who in some cases face almost saturated markets and are therefore only too happy to see competition excluded) and the larger multiple retailers who, unlike their smaller competitors, have the resources to hire the necessary experts to challenge planning decisions.

In conclusion, then, we argue against significant further regulation of retailing. We reiterate that this is an efficient and innovative industry which is of great direct and indirect importance to the UK economy; the costs of interfering with its development, or trying to reverse it, are likely considerably to exceed the benefits.

QUESTIONS FOR DISCUSSION

1. Which groups of individuals may be disadvantaged by recent retail trends? How could they be assisted without attempting to reverse these trends?

2. Why have department stores, common until the 1970s, lost out in recent years to new forms of retailing?

3. What are the issues where regulation is likely to be demanded as electronic shopping increases its market share?

4. Should competition laws allow manufacturers to refuse to supply price-cutting warehouse-based retailers on grounds of maintaining quality outlets?

5. Could we rely on competition between retailers to maintain product quality without the protection of mandatory minimum standards?

6. Is there 'excess capacity' in retailing? If so, how does it arise and need it concern us?

7. Is concentration in food retailing likely to continue to increase, or have we reached some sort of equilibrium?

8. How might we define a 'local monopoly' in retailing?

9. Would a further increase in the opening hours of shops be desirable?

10. How could retailers help to reduce the environmental impact of heavy packaging?

FURTHER READING

Bliss, C.J., 'A Theory of Retail Pricing', *Journal of Industrial Economics*, Vol.XXXVI, June 1988.

Fulop, Christina, *Revolution in Retailing*, Hobart Paper No.9, London: Institute of Economic Affairs, 1961.

Grossman, S., 'The Informational Role of Warranties and Private Disclosure about Product Quality', *Journal of Law and Economics*, Vol.24, 1981, pp.461-83.

House of Commons Environment Committee, *Shopping Centres and their Future*, London: HMSO, 1994.

International Review of Retail, Distribution and Consumer Research, London: Routledge, 1994.

Lewis, W.A., 'Competition in Retail Trade', *Economica*, New Series, Vol.12, 1945.

London Economics, *The Grocery Retailing Revolution*, 1995.

Raven, Hugh, and Tim Lang (with Caroline Dumonteil), *Off our trolleys? Food retailing and the hypermarket economy*, London: Institute for Public Policy Research, 1995.

Accountants Without Standards?

D.R. MYDDELTON

1. The stimulus for accounting regulation has often been so-called 'scandals'. Yet there is little evidence, in the UK or the USA, to show that poor or misleading disclosure has caused losses to investors.

2. The quality of UK accounting would almost certainly have improved even in the absence of accounting standards. There have indeed been some advances since 1970, but there have been disasters too: in inflation accounting, in deferred tax, in accounting for goodwill.

3. The 1948 Companies Act contained 26 pages dealing with accounts and audit; the 1985 Act (as amended) has 187 pages. In addition, UK accounting standards in issue currently total more than 600 pages; and they seem to be getting longer.

4. There is an extensive American literature on the regulation of accounting, but its outcome is remarkably inconclusive. Measuring either costs or benefits seems to be extremely difficult.

5. Preventing company directors to some extent from using their own judgement may indeed reduce 'pressure' on them; but that is not to say it will result in accounts of higher quality.

6. One can sensibly compare the financial statements of different companies only to a limited extent. Accounting standards may lead the public to expect too much in this regard.

7. There is a danger that accountants will abdicate initiative and wait for standard-setters to lay down rules. Regulations may also cause users of accounts to be irresponsible.

8. Some people assume that regulators really do know best, and want their views imposed on everyone. But there is no agreement on what is 'best', and even if there were it might not last long.

9. Permitting some choice may turn out to be a better way to improve accounting than trying to suppress dissent. In the long run monopoly provision of compulsory accounting standards may be less effective than allowing competition in ideas.

10. The direct costs of producing accounting standards are not huge. The costs of observing them are probably much higher. And their longer-term indirect disadvantages may be still more serious.

ISBN 0-255 36372-9

Hobart Paper 128

£7.60
inc. p&p

The Institute of Economic Affairs
2 Lord North Street, Westminster
London SW1P 3LB
Telephone: 0171 799 3745 Fax: 0171 799 2137

Cutting the Costs of Crime
D.J. PYLE

1. Since the end of the Second World War crime has been increasing rapidly throughout the countries of Western Europe and North America. Most crimes are committed against property.

2. Crime and its control impose considerable costs upon society. Criminal justice policy is an 'economic problem', which requires the pursuit of efficient solutions.

3. Economists argue that criminals are rational individuals who respond to incentives. In other words, criminals can be deterred by both the certainty and the severity of punishment as well as improved legitimate economic opportunities.

4. Available evidence supports the predictions of economic models of criminal participation.

5. The goal of punishment should be to minimise the costs of crime and its control.

6. In general, punishment should take the form of fines rather than imprisonment and the size of the fine should be related to the offender's wealth.

7. Penalties for crime should be structured in such a way that, when criminals can choose between a more serious and a less serious offence, they have an incentive to commit the less serious act.

8. Public sector policing has largely failed to prevent crime and to catch offenders. Individual and groups should be encouraged to purchase protection for their own neighbourhoods.

9. Individuals should be given greater financial incentives to protect their property, either through the tax system or through the insurance market.

10. The state prison system has been an expensive failure. Alternative solutions, including the greater use of non-custodial sentences and the establishment of more private prisons, should be pursued.

ISBN 0-255 36373-7

Hobart Paper 129

The Institute of Economic Affairs
2 Lord North Street, Westminster
London SW1P 3LB
Telephone: 0171 799 3745
Fax: 0171 799 2137

£6.60
inc. p&p

IEA

TAKING THE MEASURE OF POVERTY

RICHARD PRYKE

1. It is commonly believed that mass poverty has re-emerged, largely because that is the message conveyed by the DSS's *Households Below Average Income Statistics (HBAI)*.

2. But these statistics are open to serious objection. Alternative, more realistic statistics show much smaller numbers in poverty.

3. There are six major weaknesses in *HBAI*. They measure income by taking a 'snapshot', there is double-counting, they ignore the value of most goods and services provided free by the state, and the standardisation procedure for household size is dubious.

4. Particularly important, they disregard the benefits obtained from housing by owner-occupiers and those enjoying below-market rents, and they ignore the value of leisure.

5. When the DSS statistics are adjusted to provide a more appropriate measure of real income, a very different picture of poverty in Britain emerges.

6. Using the *HBAI* procedure for measuring income, between 10½ and 12 million people—around 20 per cent of the household population—were in poverty in 1988. But after adjustment to real income the number in poverty is only about 3½ million (6 per cent of the population).

7. The number in 'affluence' also declines after adjustment—from 5½ to 4 million (from 10 to 7½ per cent of the population). The wealthiest 10 per cent of the population receives less than five times as much as the poorest 10 per cent (compared with eight times before adjustment).

8. Existing *HBAI* figures are 'grossly misleading' and an '. . . economic nonsense [which] should not receive the stamp of state approval'.

9. The bulk of old-age pensioners are not poor, even if no value is placed on leisure, so there is '. . . little justification for a large or general increase in old-age pensions'.

10. In the long run, the present system of taxes and benefits seems 'unsustainable'. It is not equitable as between different income groups and involves perverse redistribution. Reform should concentrate on increasing the incentive to work rather than on reducing leisure.

ISBN 0-255 36371-0   Research Monograph 51   **£9.75** *inc. p&p*

THE INSTITUTE OF ECONOMIC AFFAIRS
2 Lord North Street, Westminster
London SW1P 3LB
Telephone: 0171-799 3745
Fax: 0171-799 2137

TAXES, BENEFITS AND FAMILY LIFE
HERMIONE PARKER

1. All income support programmes jeopardise work incentives. Yet it is important for the economy that work should be financially attractive and that extra effort and skill be rewarded.

2. Recent benefit changes and tax cuts have failed to improve work incentives for those on lower earnings.

3. A cumulative process of increasing disincentives is likely to increase the number of claimants, with the burden falling on diminishing numbers of taxpayers.

4. The tax and benefit systems also have an impact on family life. Recent changes mean that Britain is '...no longer a family-friendly country'.

5. The interaction of taxes and benefits now produces seven 'traps' – the unemployment/income support, invalidity, poverty, lone-parent, part-time, lack-of-skills, and savings traps.

6. Government under-estimates the problems of the present system and blames its victims. The issue is not so much 'scrounging': people are playing by the rules of a complex government-imposed game.

7. Spending on social security is out of control because governments which '...pay people for not working and for being "poor" end up with more people out of work and more "poor"'.

8. The present tax-benefit system should be replaced by a 'judicious combination of basic incomes (BIs: fixed amount tax credits which convert to cash for people without income to set against them) and income-tested benefits'.

9. An initial move to BIs could be made by converting personal tax allowances and child benefit into small transitional BIs – £20 a week for adults and £15·65 for children, which would cost the same as reducing the standard rate of income tax to 20%.

10. Britain's 'welfare' system is uneven between different categories of claimant and contains severe disincentives to effort. Fundamental reform is needed to remove perverse incentives which induce people to move themselves into categories where benefits are available.

ISBN 0-255 36370-2   Research Monograph 50   **£13.00** *inc. p&p*

THE INSTITUTE OF ECONOMIC AFFAIRS
2 Lord North Street, Westminster
London SW1P 3LB
Telephone: 0171 799 3745
Fax: 0171 799 2137